AFGHANISTAN

Sharifah Enayat Ali

MARSHALL CAVENDISH

New York • London • Sydney

Reference edition published 1995 by
Marshall Cavendish Corporation
99 White Plains Road
P.O. Box 2001
Tarrytown
New York 10591

© Times Editions Pte Ltd 1995

Originated and designed by
Times Books International, an imprint of
Times Editions Pte Ltd

Printed in Singapore

Library of Congress Cataloging-in-Publication Data:
Ali, Sharifah Enayat.
     Afghanistan / Sharifah Enayat Ali.
        p. cm.—(Cultures Of The World)
     Includes bibliographical references and index.
     Summary: Describes the geography, history, government,
economy, and culture of this country on the crossroads between
Europe and the Far East.
     ISBN 0-7614-0177-6 (lib. bdg.)
     1. Afghanistan—Juvenile literature. [1. Afghanistan]
I. Title. II. Series.
DS351.5.A44 1995
958.1—dc20   95–2931
                            CIP
                            AC

INTRODUCTION

AFGHANISTAN, OR "LAND OF THE AFGHANS," is a patchwork of diverse tribal kingdoms that came into existence as a single entity only in the 18th century. For millennia, this land that lies on the crossroads between Europe and the Far East, straddling the Hindu Kush mountains, has been a hive of activity. Through its passes arrived a steady stream of conquerors, adventurers, and soldiers of fortune.

Afghans are formidable fighters. They have often been called "giant killers," defeating powerful foes, including the Soviet Union and the British. Both Darius and Alexander the Great found them to be tenacious and needed to maintain strong garrisons in this region. Peace has always been elusive, for the Afghans, after driving off the interloper, inevitably fought among themselves. One thing remains constant in this turbulent country—the bold and independent spirit of its tribes.

CONTENTS

An Afghan youth wears a cloth around his head for protection against sandstorms whipped up by strong winds.

CONTENTS

Centuries-old ruins such as this one lie just outside Kabul, the capital of Afghanistan since 1776.

GEOGRAPHY

AFGHANISTAN LIES between latitudes 29° and 38°N and longitudes 61° and 75°E in southwestern Asia. With a land area of 264,000 square miles (683,760 square kilometers), it is approximately the size of Texas. Much of the country is covered by the mountain ranges of the Hindu Kush, which rises to heights of 24,000 feet (7,300 meters) in the east. In addition, there are extensive deserts and plains.

Afghanistan is landlocked. To the north lie the Central Asian republics that once belonged to the Soviet Union—Uzbekistan, Tajikistan, and Turkmenistan. Part of the boundary with these republics, about 700 miles (1,126 kilometers) long, is formed by the Oxus river, which the Afghans call the Amudar'ya. To the east and southeast, separated by the Durand Line, lies Pakistan. To the west lies Iran, while the Chinese province of Sinkiang borders the Wakhan mountains in the northeast.

Opposite: **The Band-i-Amur river, which has its source in the Hindu Kush, flows northward through the province of Balkh.**

Left: **Traversing the rugged terrain in central Afghanistan is a precarious task.**

TOPOGRAPHY

Afghanistan can broadly be divided into three regions—the northern plains, the central mountains, and the southern plateau.

NORTHERN PLAINS This region has some of the most fertile land in Afghanistan and is the country's major agricultural area. However, because rainfall is inadequate, only river valleys and regions where water is available can be cultivated.

Irrigation systems have been built along some rivers. The Kokcha and the Kunduz—two important tributaries of the Amudar'ya from the Hindu Kush—enable farmers to cultivate rice and cotton. Seminomads also raise sheep and goats on the vast grasslands here.

CENTRAL MOUNTAINS Afghanistan's mountain ranges are an extension

Rich agricultural land near Jalalabad, east of the Hindu Kush. Agriculture is the mainstay of Afghanistan's economy. Important food crops include wheat, rice, barley, and corn.

of the Himalayan mountains and cover about two-thirds of the country. The Hindu Kush, which extends across the country from the southeast to the northeast, forms the backbone of Afghanistan's central mountains.

The Kuh-e-Baba mountains, which rise to almost 17,000 feet (5,200 meters), make up the southwestern branch of the Hindu Kush. The highest mountain here is the Shah Fuladi (16,873 feet or 5,141 meters). The highest peaks in Afghanistan, however, are found near the northeastern border with Pakistan, where the Nowshak (24,557 feet or 7,482 meters), the country's highest mountain, is located. The northeastern part of the highlands, including the Wakhan, is geologically active. In this century alone, more than a dozen earthquakes have occurred in the area around Kabul.

The 320-mile (515-kilometer) Kabul river is a vital source of water here, as its tributaries irrigate some of the most productive agricultural land in the country. To the east, the Khyber Pass enables travelers to traverse the daunting terrain of the Hindu Kush into Pakistan. Another mountain route, the Baroghil Pass, links the Wakhan with northern Pakistan.

The Helmand is the longest river flowing entirely within Afghanistan. It is about 700 miles (1,126 kilometers) long, and together with its tributaries, drains the whole of southern Afghanistan. The Amudar'ya, which forms part of the boundary between Afghanistan and the Central Asian republics, is the major river in the north. Rising in the Hindu Kush, it flows for 1,500 miles (2,414 kilometers) to empty into the Aral Sea in Turkmenistan.

SOUTHERN PLATEAU The southwestern region consists primarily of desert and semidesert. The largest deserts here are the Registan, Dasht-i-Margo, and Dasht-i-Khash. These barren areas, which cover over 40,000 square miles (103,600 square kilometers), lie between 1,500 and 2,000 feet (450 and 600 meters) above sea level. The entire region is bisected by the Helmand river, which flows from the Hindu Kush to Lake Helmand, a vast, marshy lake in Sistan Basin on the Iranian border. Lake Helmand, one of the few lakes in Afghanistan, expands and contracts with the seasonal flow of its rivers. In the extreme southwest is the marshland of Gaud-i-Zirreh.

CLIMATE

Severe winters and long, hot summers characterize Afghanistan's climate. The climate is influenced more by high altitude than by latitude. From December to March, the air masses come from the cold continental north, bringing very cold weather and snow to the mountains.

The months from June to September are very hot and dry, although eastern Afghanistan receives some rain from a weakened monsoon. However, even in summer, nights can be very cold. Very little rain falls at lower altitudes, and the plains are extremely dry. Rainfall in the country averages just seven inches (18 cm) a year. The southwest is even more arid. Strong winds, such as the *bad-i-sad-o-bist-roz* ("bawh-dee-sah-doh-bist-ROHZ") along the Iran-Afghanistan border, commonly cause sandstorms. In the southwestern deserts, the temperature difference between day and night can be very extreme. In the summer, water freezes at night, despite noon temperatures of up 120°F (49°C).

Only in areas like Kabul, which are at higher altitudes and are sheltered, is the climate relatively pleasant. Kabul's yearly temperature ranges between 23°F and 77°F (−5°C and 25°C).

FLORA AND FAUNA

Less than 1% of Afghanistan is forested. The forests thrive mainly in the mountains and include pine, cypress, oak, juniper, laurel, barberry, hazelnut, and wild almond. The most prized tree is the deodar, a cedar that Afghans use to build furniture and houses. Stunted pines and oaks are also much sought after by woodcutters. In the spring, flowers such as the cowslip and anemone bloom in the valleys and hillsides. As summer approaches, tulips appear, followed by petunias, sunflowers, marigolds, honeysuckle, dahlias, and geraniums.

In the Hindu Kush, the animals are typical of the nearby Himalayas. They include the snow cock, ibex, brown bear, snow leopard, piping hare, and sometimes even the Siberian tiger. The northern plains have the fauna of the steppes, such as bustards and the suslik, a ground squirrel. In the western deserts roam the creatures characteristic of the Caspian—gazelle, coursers, flamingos, and swallow plovers. Camels are native to the region: the single-humped dromedary is common on the plains, and the double-

The vegetation on the Hindu Kush provides sufficient grazing for flocks of sheep, seen here moving along narrow mountain paths.

humped Bactrian camel is found in the mountains. Wild pigs, which the Afghans call *jangal* ("jehng-EHL"), are also found in the tamarisk groves.

The cheetah, leopard, mongoose, and other animals of the Indian subcontinent are found in south and eastern Afghanistan. The macaque is found in the forested areas of Nuristan, near the Pakistani border. Leopards, otters, and foxes are sometimes hunted for their pelts, which are sold as blankets and coats.

Fish abound in the rivers. To the north of the Hindu Kush, a trout called *mahi-kholdar* ("maw-hee-KHOOL-darh"), is found. Barbels and carp thrive in all the waters, as does a tasty but bony fish called *shir-mahi* ("shuhr-MAW-HEE"), or milk fish. Freshwater crabs and small fish, such as minnows, help to keep the streams clean.

Eighty species of doves and pigeons populate the plains and foothills of Afghanistan. Nightingales can be heard in the summer, and jays, magpies, pipits, larks, and crows are also plentiful. Falcons, eagles, and vultures are sometimes seen patrolling the skies on the lookout for prey. Many species of game birds are found, including the chukar partridge, with its distinctive red bill and legs. The size of a small chicken, it is hunted for food and bred for fighting.

Camels are bred for transportation in Afghanistan, especially by the nomadic peoples.

CITIES

KABUL From Kabul, the capital of Afghanistan, roads lead in all directions. There are roads through the gorges of the Hindu Kush leading north to the Amudar'ya and the northern plains, roads east through the Khyber Pass to India, south to Pakistan and the sea through Ghazni and Kandahar, and west to Herat and Iran.

Throughout the ages, Kabul has been an important city because of its strategic location at the center of these vital crossroads. In the 19th century, Kabul was twice captured by the British during the Anglo-Afghan wars. Nestling 6,000 feet (1,828 meters) above sea level, on a well-sheltered plateau, Kabul is the largest city in the country, with an estimated population of about two million.

Bare rocky mountains rise in the south and west. Because of the altitude, Kabul's climate is not unlike that of Denver, Colorado—invigorating, with brilliant sunshine and thin, clear air. The summers are dry, with rain in spring and heavy snowfall in the winter, when the city is often snowbound.

For centuries, Kabul has stood in the path of great invaders, from Alexander the Great and Genghis Khan to Tamerlane and Nadir Shah.

13

A crowded bazaar in one of the older sections of Kabul. Transactions are carried out in the local currency, the afghani.

In Kabul the contrast between the old and new can be very sharp. On the south bank of the Kabul river are parts of the old city, a collection of flat-roofed houses packed closely together. Found here are covered bazaars and narrow alleys, brimming with everything residents need, from exotic carpets to nuts, fruits, grains, and various kinds of handicrafts and garments.

Many of the old bazaars have been torn down to build modern two- and three-storied buildings of apartments over shops. The boulevards in the newer sections of Kabul are broad and paved with asphalt. They carry an incredible mixture of traffic: trucks, buses, jeeps, and automobiles move alongside camels, donkeys, and horse carts—all laden high with an array of goods and passengers. Many sections of Kabul were destroyed or damaged during the Soviet occupation and the factional fighting that erupted after the Soviet troops pulled out.

KANDAHAR Kandahar is the capital of Kandahar province, one of the richest provinces in Afghanistan. Fruits and large quantities of wool are produced in the region around the city.

Kandahar was the first capital of modern Afghanistan. It has wide, cobbled main streets. Unlike Kabul, its bazaars are roomy and open. The houses have arched doorways and are made of baked bricks laid over wooden scaffolding, which is used over and over again as wood is scarce.

The city is free of winter snow and lies on the shortest air route between Europe and Asia. It also has an international airport. An excellent road, which is open in all weather, connects the city to Pakistan.

MAZAR-E-SHARIF Mazar-e-Sharif is the largest city in northern Afghanistan. It is an important trading center for the north and lies just 13 miles (21 kilometers) southwest of the Amudar'ya. It is best known throughout the Islamic world as the site of the tomb of Ali, the son-in-law of the Prophet Mohammed.

GHAZNI Ghazni, which lies 80 miles (129 kilometers) south of Kabul, was the resplendent capital of Mahmud Shah, a ruler of the Ghazni dynasty, in the 11th century. Today it is an important commercial center.

HERAT Herat is situated in the Hari Rud valley, a major fruit and grain producing area in western Afghanistan. Its proximity to Iran made it the center for Persian art and architecture during the 15th and 16th centuries. The old city is surrounded by a large moat and massive walls with many towers. Today, a modern area has grown around the walls. Herat is famous for its carpets and woolen cloth.

The civil war of the last 15 years has caused major shifts in the population of Afghanistan's towns and cities. In the mid-1980s, Herat, for example, lost almost two-thirds of its population as residents fled the war-torn city.

HISTORY

IT WAS ONLY as recently as 1747 that Afghanistan as we know it today emerged as a nation. This rugged land, which lies on the crossroads between Europe and China, has a long and turbulent history of warfare and invasion. The Persians, Greeks, Mongols, British, and Russians have, at various times, conquered and occupied Afghanistan.

EARLY CIVILIZATION

Archeological finds since 1949 reveal that humans had settled in northern Afghanistan some 50,000 years ago. Historians also believe that Afghanistan may have been one

Above: **The citadel of Alexander the Great in Herat.**

Opposite: **A 174-foot (53-meter) statue of Buddha in Bamian, built during the period when Buddhism was a primary religion in northern Afghanistan.**

of the areas where humans first domesticated animals and plants, such as wheat and barley.

Research also suggests that the agricultural villages that provided food supplies to Mahenjo-Daro, Harappa, and the other great regional centers of the Indus valley civilizations may have been in Afghanistan.

ACHAEMENID EMPIRE

The ancient land of Bactria in northern Afghanistan first appeared in recorded history when it was conquered by the Persian monarch Cyrus the Great about 540 B.C. and incorporated into his Achaemenid empire.

Darius the Great and Xerxes further expanded the empire to include several satrapies (Persian provinces) in and around Afghanistan, creating the largest empire of the ancient world.

GREEK RULE

As a young man, from age 13 to 16, Alexander the Great was taught by the philosopher Aristotle.

In 336 B.C., Alexander the Great succeeded to the throne of Macedonia and began his military campaign against the Achaemenid empire. He defeated the Persians in 330 B.C. and entered the Hindu Kush a year later. After capturing Herat, he moved on to Sistan and later marched into what is today Kandahar. From here he continued up the Arghandab valley, from Ghazni across the watershed to the Kabul valley.

In 328 B.C., Alexander marched his army north through the Hindu Kush passes and spent a year conquering the land on both sides of the Amudar'ya river.

After Alexander's death in 323 B.C., Bactria became part of the Seleucid empire, founded by one of Alexander's generals, Seleucus. Much of the land south of the Hindu Kush fell under the control of Chandragupta, who had established the Mauryan empire in northern India. Chandragupta's successor, Asoka, was a devout apostle of Buddhism and established several important religious centers in the Hindu Kush.

In 185 B.C., the Mauryan empire broke up. The Greeks in the north, who had by then established an independent Greco-Bactrian kingdom, quickly took advantage and moved south across the Hindu Kush.

THE ROMANCE OF ALEXANDER AND ROXANE

Among Alexander the Great's prisoners was the beautiful Roxane, the daughter of Oyartes, a leader of Bactria. Legend has it that Alexander fell in love with Roxane and married her in a part-Persian, part-Macedonian ceremony.

The Afghans are very fond of this romance, and Afghan folklore is filled with stories about it. Even today, many baby girls are named Roxane.

However, the Bactrian empire itself was soon weakened by internal strife and pressure from the nomads of the north and broke up. Greek rule in Afghanistan had ended, but their influence on art and culture remained. The combination of Grecian, Mauryan, and Kushan cultures produced what is today known as Gandharan art, found in the cities and monasteries of the Kabul valley.

SUCCESSION OF CONQUERORS

The Saka were the nomadic invaders from Central Asia who pushed the Greeks out of Bactria and northwest India. The Saka occupied Sakastan (modern Sistan) and for a short time ruled the land between the Helmand river and the Persian Gulf. Then the Parthians, who controlled Iran, conquered Sakastan and made it a Parthian satrapy. At its peak, the Parthian-ruled empire extended from Armenia to India.

The Parthians were, in turn, overthrown by the Kushans from across the Amudar'ya. By the middle of first century A.D., the Kushans had crossed the Hindu Kush and were ruling the entire Kabul valley, which was known as Gandhara. The Kushans controlled all the land from the lower Indus valley to the Iranian border and from the Chinese Sinkiang to the Caspian and Aral seas.

Kanishka was the greatest of the Kushan emperors. During his reign, Buddhism enjoyed its greatest influence and spread to the Far East and parts of Southeast Asia. Sculpture and art also flourished and made a great impact on the cultures of Afghanistan, India, Iran, and even China. The Kushan dynasty ended in A.D. 220, and the country became fragmented.

In the third century A.D., Ardashir founded the mighty Sassanian dynasty, which ruled over the Persian empire for four centuries, dominating Afghanistan and Pakistan west of the Indus.

The most important archeological find in Afghanistan was made in 1963 when the French located the Greek city at Ai Khanoum, at the confluence of the Kokcha and Darya-i-Panj rivers. This is the easternmost Greek city ever discovered and consists of several complexes. The upper town has a huge citadel, and the lower town has residential and administrative buildings, including a palace, a university, a gymnasium, and a temple.

ASOKA'S ROCK AND PILLAR OF EDICTS

Archeological evidence confirming the truth of the historical references to the lands of the Hindu Kush have grown steadily since World War II. Asoka's Rock and Pillar of Edicts, for example, were found in 1958 and 1963, respectively, near Kandahar.

The Rock and Pillar of Edicts were Asoka's way of educating his subjects into adopting the Buddhist way of life of nonviolence and teaching them moral values. They were very much like the billboards in the United States today; only, he was advertising a way of life, instead of a product.

The Edicts revealed several important facts. They have Greek and Aramaic text. Aramaic was the official language of the Achaemenid empire and the main language for most of western Asia before it was replaced by Greek and local Iranian languages.

The Edicts show that Aramaic still existed, long after the fall of the Achaemenid empire. They also show the importance of Greek in the Afghan region. The Edicts also testify to the existence of humanitarian values.

COMING OF ISLAM

In some ways, the Islamic conquest of Afghanistan has lasted to this day. The Arabs defeated the Sassanids in Persia about A.D. 642, bringing Iran under Arab control. In 652, the governor of Basra sent an expedition to invade Sistan and then on to Kabul to punish the king, who had refused to pay tribute. The Arabs crossed the Amudar'ya in 667 and invaded Herat. By 714, Arab control of the region up to the Indus river was complete.

During the caliphate of Harun al-Rashid of the Abbasid dynasty, Balkh became a great seat of learning. In the ninth century, the Abbasids were displaced by three local kingdoms in quick succession—the Tahirids, Saffarids, and Samanids. The Saffarids were the first to unite the regions north and south of the Hindu Kush under one rule. They were instrumental in converting the remote tribes to Islam and in promoting the use of Farsi (the language of Persia) among the people.

The Samanids overthrew the Saffarids and by 920 had established a great empire that stretched from India to Baghdad. By 943, this empire had begun to decay, and the kings' Turkish slaves increased their influence over their masters.

The Ghazni Victory Tower was built by Mahmud of Ghazni to commemorate his military victories.

GHAZNAVID DYNASTY

In 962, one of these slaves, Alptigin, overthrew his master and became ruler of Ghazni—thus founding the Ghaznavid dynasty, which brought an era of magnificence to this region. The third ruler of this dynasty, Mahmud of Ghazni, contributed tremendously to the expansion of Islam in the region and India. In addition to being a great general, he was a patron of the arts and filled his capital, Ghazni, and other cities with the best intellectuals, artists, and scientists of his time.

Among them were the poet Firdausi, scientist-historian al-Biruni, and the historian al-Utbi. Mahmud used Afghan mercenaries in his conquest of India, where they not only succeeded to the throne of Delhi and the command of three important principalities but also were renowned in India for the next 300 years for their military prowess.

After Mahmud's death in 1030, the empire declined and was finally overthrown by the Ghorids from northwestern Afghanistan, who captured and burned the splendid city of Ghazni to the ground. The Ghorids went on to conquer India and almost forgot their homeland.

During Tamerlane's rule, Herat became a renowned center of art and learning throughout the Muslim world.

MONGOL RULE

In the 13th century, Genghis Khan swept out of Central Asia with his Mongolian forces and mercilessly destroyed everything in his path—cities, commercial centers, shrines, monuments, crops, irrigation systems, and people. He left ruin and desolation wherever he passed.

In 1220, Genghis Khan reached the Amudar'ya and destroyed Balkh and Herat. Returning from India, he ordered Ghazni destroyed and finally left the region in 1223, leaving behind vast expanses of rubble, sand-filled irrigation canals and wells, and fields that had once been cultivated. Some of this devastation left scars that have never healed. Buddhism was almost totally dislodged from the region. Islam had gained a much stronger foothold and continued to flourish.

By the middle of the 14th century, Mongol rule had lost much of its hold, and the only traces left were the few colonies, such as the Hazaras, that they had established. Both Marco Polo and Ibn-Battuta passed through this region during this era and have left records of their observations.

Between 1332 and 1370, this region was ruled independently by the Kurds of Herat, who were descended from the Ghorids, until the arrival of Tamerlane, a descendant of Genghis Khan. On his route to India, Tamerlane passed over the Hindu Kush, laying to waste everything in his path; this destruction is evident to this day in the dry waste of the Helmand valley.

Unlike Genghis Khan, however, Tamerlane had a humane side. Tamerlane was a patron of the arts, organized administration, constructed public works, and encouraged commerce and industry, introducing new trade routes. Tamerlane's Timurid dynasty, with a capital in Herat, lasted for about 100 years: it was a prosperous period for Afghanistan.

When Tamerlane's empire shrank, several local chieftains took over different parts of the region. One of them, Buhlul Lodi, captured the throne at Delhi and founded the Lodi dynasty, which lasted for just 75 years. His power, however, encouraged many Afghans to move to India, where they were eventually absorbed into the local population.

Babur, a Timurid prince and a descendant of Genghis Khan, lost his kingdom of Farghana to the Uzbeks. Dejected, he set out with a few followers on a journey that ended in the founding of the great Moghul empire of India.

Babur had a very special affection for Kabul; he found its scenery and climate delightful and made the city his capital until 1526, when he moved to Delhi. Delhi's strategic and economic importance made it easier for him to administer his huge empire from there.

The Moghul armies depended heavily on the Afghan tribes of the Sulaiman mountains. Eventually, these tribes played a major role in the disintegration of the Moghul empire, masterfully pitting the Persians and the Moghuls against each other in their struggle to control the strategic areas of the mountain crossroads.

For a while, the Ghilzai Pushtuns, under the leadership of a general called Mir Wais Khan, overthrew the Persians and took control of a large part of the Persian empire. However, because of internal disputes and jealousies, they lost not only Persia but also Kandahar to Nadir Shah, a Turkish tribes member from Khorasan.

After defeating the Pushtuns near Jalalabad, Nadir Shah marched through the Khyber Pass to Delhi. Among the treasures he looted from Delhi were the Peacock Throne and the Koh-i-Noor diamond.

Babur was a poet of considerable gifts. His prose memoirs, the Babur-nameh, *originally written in Turkic, were later translated into Farsi and then English in the 20th century. After making Delhi his capital, he never returned to Kabul during the remainder of his lifetime but asked to be buried there.*

Ahmad Shah made Kandahar the capital of his empire. In 1776, three years after his death, the capital was moved to Kabul by his successors.

BIRTH OF THE AFGHAN STATE

Ahmad Khan Sadozai was a Pushtun chief of the Abdali tribe who was an officer in Nadir Shah's army. The night Nadir Shah was assassinated, Ahmad Khan fought his way out of the Persian camp, seized a convoy carrying treasure (including the Koh-i-Noor diamond), and marched to Kandahar.

In 1747, the Afghans announced that they no longer owed allegiance to Persia and declared independence under Ahmad Khan, who took on the title of Ahmad Shah.

Over the next 26 years, Ahmad Shah created a single Afghanistan out of what until then had been distinctly different regions ruled by diverse foreign powers or local chiefs. He took the title of *Durr-i-Durrani* ("DOO-ree-DOO-RAH-ni"), or pearl of pearls.

Ahmad Shah went on to seize all the territories west of the Indus from Kashmir to the Arabian Sea. In 1761, when he defeated the Mahrattas in India, his empire reached its zenith.

He ruled through a council of chiefs, with each chief responsible for his own tribe. This system, which carried on the traditional role of the chief as first among equals, won the support of the people.

Within 40 years of his death in 1773, Ahmad Shah's empire fell apart. Bickering and jealousies among his successors led to the downfall of the ruling family. His son Timur Shah had 23 sons and died without naming an heir, and for a quarter of a century after this, the Durrani princes intrigued and plotted against one another.

When the princes executed the chieftain of the rival Mohamadzai tribe and blinded his eldest son, the tribe rebelled. The dead chieftain's youngest son, Dost Mohammed Khan, defeated the Durrani ruler near Kabul.

ARRIVAL OF WESTERN POWERS

By this time very little of the Durrani kingdom was left, and when the Sikhs began pressing their claims to Peshawar, Dost Mohammed asked the British for help. The British in India were moving north at the same time as the Russians were moving south into Central Asia. As only the land in the Hindu Kush remained between these powers, Afghanistan became a pawn between them. When the British refused to support Afghan claims in the Punjab, Dost Mohammed turned to the Czar of Russia for help.

The British invaded Afghanistan, precipitating the First Afghan War (1838–1842), and captured Kandahar and Ghazni. Dost Mohammed fled, and the British put Shah Shuja, a puppet monarch, on the throne and garrisoned Kabul. The Afghans rebelled, and the harassed British garrison were forced to evacuate Kabul. Although the Afghan leaders in Kabul promised safe passage, this promise carried little weight with the tribes. The British column was massacred before it could reach Jalalabad, and according to some reports, only one man survived.

Afghan warriors in 1878. William Gladstone, British Prime Minister four times between 1868 and 1894, later called the Second Afghan War "the most frivolous war ever waged."

Shah Shuja was assassinated by the Afghans, and Dost Mohammed returned to Afghanistan. Before he died in 1863, he managed to unify Afghanistan. Dost Mohammed was succeeded by his son Sher Ali.

The Russians, having moved their troops to the Afghan border in 1878, sent a diplomatic mission to Afghanistan. When the British sent a counter mission, the group was stopped by border guards. The British demanded an apology; not satisfied by Sher Ali's explanation, they invaded Afghanistan in December 1878. The resulting conflict was the Second Afghan War. Sher Ali fled north, seeking Russian help. He was unsuccessful and died at Mazar-e-Sharif.

The British placed his son Yakub Khan in charge; he agreed to all British demands, including the acceptance of a British advisor. Yakub Khan was unacceptable to the Afghans. They assassinated the British representatives, and the British army occupied Kabul and Kandahar. Yakub Khan fled to India.

The British were constantly attacked by the tribes. They eventually relinquished Afghanistan to Abdur Rahman, a grandson of Dost Mohammed, but continued to manage Afghanistan's foreign affairs. The Durand Line was defined to mark the boundary between British India and Afghanistan. The line cut through the region inhabited by the Pushtuns and has been a source of contention ever since. Abdur Rahman was forced to accept as part of Afghanistan the Wakhan Corridor (the region covered by the Wakhan range), which was designed to form a buffer between Russia and British India. Reluctantly, he took on the responsibility of controlling the Kirghiz bandits in the Wakhan.

The British drove Dost Mohammed (*below*) from his throne in 1839, but reinstated him in 1842. Dost Mohammed allied himself with the British against the Persians in 1857.

MOVES TOWARD MODERNIZATION

Abdur Rahman's first task was to unite the country—he tried to reduce the power of the various tribes by shifting more power to the central government. He also practiced a policy of isolation by not granting concessions to any foreign powers. His son, Habibullah, introduced Western medicine, abolished slavery, and founded colleges based on those in Europe.

During World War I, Afghanistan remained neutral, despite pressure from its neighbors. When Habibullah was assassinated, his son Amanullah assumed control. To gain complete independence from Britain, Amanullah attacked British troops in India, beginning the Third Afghan War. In the peace treaty signed in Rawalpindi in 1921, Britain relinquished control over Afghanistan's foreign policy.

Amanullah angered the conservative families and the *mullahs* ("mool-LAHs"), or Muslim clerics, by introducing drastic reforms to modernize Afghanistan. He abolished the *purdah* ("perhr-DAH"), or the wearing of a face-concealing veil for women, opened coeducational schools, introduced Western dress, and started a program to educate the nomads.

Resentment against modernization grew. In 1928, the tribes revolted and Amanullah was overthrown. After nine months of chaos, Nadir Khan, the great-grandson of one of Dost Mohammed's brothers, emerged to take control. An assembly of tribal chiefs proclaimed him Nadir Shah, king of Afghanistan.

Nadir Shah based his administration on orthodox Islamic law and set up the *Loya Jirgah* ("Law-yah jorhr-GAH," or Great Assembly), representing all the tribes. From it a National Council was formed. An upper house consisting of "intellectuals" was also created. Political parties, however, were not allowed.

One of Nadir Shah's more notable achievements was the construction of a road through the Shibar Pass to the north of the Hindu Kush. He also promoted a policy of friendly relations with foreign powers and the extension of educational facilities, including public schools and a military academy.

Zahir Shah, the last king of Afghanistan. He was in Italy when Daoud Khan overthrew the monarchy in July 1973.

Nadir Shah abolished some of the reforms of Amanullah that had angered the conservative elements, and women returned to the *purdah*. In 1933, Nadir Shah was assassinated. His son Zahir Shah was then proclaimed king. During World War II, Afghanistan remained neutral and emerged relatively unscathed from the war. In 1953, Daoud Khan, Zahir Shah's cousin, took over as prime minister. He secured aid from the Soviet Union and began plans to modernize the country. However, he was dismissed in 1963.

Zahir Shah signed a new democratic constitution into law in 1964, with a fully elected lower house and a partly elected upper house. Political parties were still not allowed to operate. In 1973, Daoud reappeared and overthrew Zahir Shah in a bloodless coup. Afghanistan was declared a republic. Daoud banned all political parties to strengthen his hold over the country.

In 1978, Daoud was killed in a coup after attempting to crack down on his political foes. This came to be known as the Saur Revolution. Leaders of the communist People's Democratic Party of Afghanistan (PDPA) assumed control of the country. Nur Mohammed Taraki became the president of the Revolutionary Council and prime minister of Afghanistan. Babrak Karmal was chosen to be deputy prime minister.

The PDPA was divided into two factions, the Khalq, led by Hafizullah Amin and Taraki, and the Parcham, led by Karmal. Old conflicts between the factions erupted anew. Thousands of people were killed or imprisoned without trial, and sweeping land reforms and radical social changes were decreed. The black, red, and green Islamic flag was replaced by a red communist one.

SOVIET INVASION

Armed resistance to the communist regime, which soon developed into guerrilla warfare, mounted during the winter of 1978. Desertion by Afghan soldiers grew as Soviet advisors tightened their hold over the army, and a network of guerrilla training camps developed in Pakistan and Iran.

In October 1979, Hafizullah Amin had Taraki killed when it became clear that Taraki, with Soviet backing, was plotting to remove him from power. Amin's days, however, were numbered. On Christmas Eve, 1979, Soviet troops began landing at Kabul airport, launching an invasion of Afghanistan. Afghan troops were no match for the well-armed Soviets, and Amin was killed. Babrak Karmal was set up as president.

The Muslim tribes united into the *mujahedin* ("moo-JAH-hee-DEEN") resistance movement and waged a fierce guerrilla war financed by Pakistan and the United States. Despite their vastly superior arms and resources, the Soviets were unable to defeat the mountain-based rebels. In 1986, Karmal was replaced by Sayid Mohammed Najibullah.

By 1988, there were some 115,000 Soviet troops stationed in Afghanistan. Many countries, including the United States, boycotted the 1980 Summer Olympic Games in Moscow in protest against the Soviet invasion.

29

When the *mujahedin* began their struggle against the Soviets, they were poorly armed. From 1984, however, increasingly sophisticated weapons were supplied by the United States, Britain, and China.

When Mikhail Gorbachev came to power in the Soviet Union in 1985, he began moves to end his country's intervention in Afghanistan. The war was unpopular with the Soviet public and its costs placed a heavy burden on the Soviet economy. It was also damaging to the Soviet Union's relations with Muslim countries.

In April 1988, a ceasefire was declared after Afghanistan, Pakistan, the Soviet Union, and the United States concluded a series of agreements in Geneva for a Soviet troop withdrawal. The withdrawal began in May 1988 and was completed in February 1989, leaving the cities in the hands of a pro-Moscow government and the countryside in the hands of the *mujahedin*. Both the Soviet Union and the United States, however, continued to send weapons into Afghanistan.

The communist regime of Najibullah survived another three years before being overthrown by the *mujahedin* in April 1992. Najibullah, unable to flee Kabul, took refuge at the United Nations compound. Rival *mujahedin* leaders and parties then continued struggling for supremacy.

POWER STRUGGLE CONTINUES

General Abdul Rashid Dostum, the Uzbek militia leader and northern warlord, who had previously been deployed by Najibullah against the rebel forces, defected to the *mujahedin* units under the command of Ahmed Shah Massoud, a Tajik commander fighting under the banner of Burhanuddin Rabbani's Jamiat-i-Islami group. The other major *mujahedin* leader was Gulbuddin Hekmatyar, the Pushtun leader of one faction of the fundamentalist Hezb-i-Islam.

As the three factions congregated in and around Kabul in April 1992, fighting erupted between the forces of Hekmatyar and Massoud (supported by Dostum). The Hezb-i-Wadat group of the predominantly Shi'ite Hazara tribe was also heavily involved in the fighting in and around Kabul throughout the year. Although the Islamic state of Afghanistan was established soon after this, conflicts continued to occur.

Gulbuddin Hekmatyar, one of the players in the power struggle in Afghanistan. His main backing is from commanders among the Pushtuns, who form the country's largest ethnic group.

REFUGEES: CASUALTIES OF WAR

By the end of 1987, an estimated 9% of the population of Afghanistan had been killed.

More than 3.5 million Afghans became refugees in Pakistan, 2.4 million in Iran, and 3 million more in their own country. Of these, by December 1993, over 2 million had returned to their war-torn country. Dangers from the renewed conflict have deterred more refugees from returning home. Many Afghans have also fallen victim to landmines, which were laid by the Soviet army.

GOVERNMENT

THE GOVERNMENT OF AFGHANISTAN has undergone several radical changes in the last two decades. In 1973, the constitutional monarchy of Zahir Shah was overthrown by Daoud Khan. Afghanistan was declared a republic the following year.

Communism took a foothold in 1978 after Daoud was killed in a coup. In 1992, Najibullah's Soviet-backed regime collapsed, and the Islamic state of Afghanistan was proclaimed.

On New Year's Day 1994, hostilities again broke out in Kabul and the northern provinces as rival *mujahedin* groups jostled for power in the country. Among the major players in the power struggle are President Burhanuddin Rabbani, his main rival Prime Minister Gulbuddin Hekmatyar, Defense Minister Ahmed Shah Massoud (who has aligned himself with Rabbani), and General Abdul Rashid Dostum, whose sudden defection from Rabbani's side to join Hekmatyar sparked off the war.

Above: **Former President Najibullah.**

Opposite: **In the present political chaos in Afghanistan, soldiers and guns are the most potent form of power.**

POLITICAL SYSTEM

Afghanistan has been an Islamic state since April 1992, following 14 years of civil war. Under a plan agreed to by moderate Sunni *mujahedin* groups on April 24, 1992, a 51-member Islamic Jihad Council, headed by Seghbatullah Mujaddedi, took control for a period of two months. Shortly afterward, an interim legislative body, known as the Leadership Council, headed by Burhanuddin Rabbani, was formed.

On June 28, Mujaddedi ended his term as acting president, handing over power to the multifaction interim government of Rabbani. On December 30, a newly created Constituent Assembly elected Rabbani as president for a two-year term. The assembly also appointed a parliament.

THE CONSTITUTION

Immediately after the Saur Revolution, the 1977 constitution was abolished. Both Nur Mohammed Taraki and his successor Hafizullah Amin promised to draw up a new constitution, but they were removed from power before any drafts could be drawn up by the special commissions they had appointed.

In 1980, the Revolutionary Council ratified the Basic Principles of the Democratic Republic of Afghanistan. These were superseded by a new constitution ratified in April 1985. In 1987, the *Loya Jirgah* ratified another constitution, which was later amended in 1990.

Following the downfall of Najibullah's regime in April 1992, the Leadership Council appointed a commission to draw up a new and more strictly Islamic constitution. By this constitution, no law is allowed to run counter to the principles of Islam. The civil war that broke out on New Year's Day 1994 has, however, disrupted this work.

LOYA JIRGAH

The *Loya Jirgah* is the most powerful legislative body in Afghanistan. It is composed of:
- the president and the vice-presidents;
- members of the *Meli Shura* ("MEH-li SHOO-rah"), or National Assembly;
- the general prosecutor;
- the Council of Ministers;

- the attorney-general, his or her deputies, and members of the attorney-general's office;
- the chairperson of the Constitution Council;
- the heads of the provincial councils;
- representatives from each province, according to the number of their representatives in the *Wolasi Jirgah* ("woo-LAW-si jorhr-GAH"), or House of Representatives, elected by the people in a general secret ballot;
- a minimum of 50 people from among prominent political, scientific, social, and religious figures appointed by the president.

The *Loya Jirgah* is empowered to approve and amend the constitution; to elect the president and to accept the resignation of the president; to consent to the declaration of war and armistice; and to adopt decisions on major questions regarding the destiny of the country.

Decisions are adopted by a majority vote. In the event of the dissolution of the *Wolasi Jirgah*, its members retain their membership of the *Loya Jirgah* until a new *Wolasi Jirgah* is elected.

The Ministry of Interior building, Kabul. This ministry is one of 22 ministries in the Afghan government.

THE PRESIDENT

The president is the head of state and, according to the 1990 constitution, is elected by a majority vote of the *Loya Jirgah* for a term of seven years. Any Muslim citizen of Afghanistan who is more than 40 years of age can be elected president. No person is allowed to serve for more than two terms.

The president exercises a wide range of executive powers. He or she ratifies the resolutions of the *Meli Shura*, appoints the prime minister, and approves the appointment of the ministers, judges, and army officials. The president is the supreme commander of the armed forces and can proclaim a state of emergency or declare war, with the consent of the *Loya Jirgah*. The president is accountable and reports to the *Loya Jirgah*.

MELI SHURA

The *Meli Shura* is the highest legislative body of Afghanistan. It consists of two houses: the *Wolasi Jirgah* (House of Representatives) and the *Sena* ("SI-nah"), or Senate.

Members of the *Wolasi Jirgah* are elected by secret ballot by the general populace for a term of five years. Members of the *Sena* are elected and appointed in a different manner—two people from each province are elected by the provincial council for a period of three years; the remaining one-third of the senators are appointed by the president for a term of four years.

The *Meli Shura* is vested with the authority to approve, amend, and repeal laws and legislative decrees; to interpret laws; to ratify and annul international treaties; to approve socioeconomic development plans; and to approve the state budget.

It also has the authority to establish and make changes to administrative units; to establish and abolish ministries; to appoint and remove vice-presidents on the recommendation of the president; and to endorse the establishment of relations with foreign countries and international organizations.

The *Wolasi Jirgah* also has the power to approve a vote of confidence or no confidence on the Council of Ministers or one of its member bodies. At its first session, the *Wolasi Jirgah* elects, from among its members, an executive committee headed by a chairperson for the whole term of the legislature. The *Sena* elects, from among its members, an executive committee composed of a chairperson for a term of five years and two deputy chairpersons and two secretaries, for a term of one year.

If the decision of one house is rejected by the other, a joint committee, consisting of an equal number of members from both houses, can be formed. A decision by the joint committee agreed upon by a two-thirds majority will be considered valid after approval by the president. If the joint committee fails to resolve differences, the matter is discussed in a joint session of the *Meli Shura*, and a decision is reached by a majority vote.

The Afghan army disintegrated into factional groups after President Najibullah was ousted. At the time, its equipment included about 1,200 battle tanks.

The police headquarters in Kabul. Following the collapse of Najibullah's government, the police security forces, together with all the military bodies of the former communist regime, were combined with the *mujahedin* forces to form a new national Islamic military force.

COUNCIL OF MINISTERS

The Council of Ministers is composed of a prime minister, deputy prime ministers, and ministers. The Council of Ministers is appointed by the prime minister. The present prime minister of Afghanistan is Gulbuddin Hekmatyar, who accepted the position in March 1993, and was sworn in as head of a coalition government in July 1993.

The Council of Ministers formulates and implements domestic and foreign policies and formulates economic development plans and the state budget.

THE CONSTITUTION COUNCIL

The Constitution Council evaluates and ensures the conformity of laws, legislative decrees, and international treaties with the constitution. It also gives legal advice to the prime minister on constitutional matters.

The Constitution Council is composed of a chairperson, a vice-chairperson, and eight members, who are appointed by the president.

THE JUDICIAL SYSTEM

The functions and structure of the judiciary are established in the constitution ratified by the *Loya Jirgah* in November 1987 and amended in May 1990.

The courts apply the provisions of the constitution and the laws of Afghanistan, and in the case of ambivalence, judges in accordance with the laws of *Shariah* ("SHAH-ri-yah," the Islamic legal system). Trials are held in open sessions and are conducted in Pushtu and Dari or in the language of the majority of the inhabitants of that locality. The judiciary has two levels, the Supreme Court and the lower courts. The state can also establish specialized courts within the unified system of the judiciary.

The highest judicial body is the Supreme Court, which consists of the chief justice and judges, all of whom are appointed by the president. It supervises the judicial activities of the courts and ensures the uniformity of law enforcement and interpretations of those courts. Death sentences are carried out after ratification by the president.

The *mujahedin* government, in April 1992, in an apparent attempt to improve security in Kabul, established special courts to prosecute people who violate homes, honor, children, or property.

The national flag of Afghanistan has three equal horizontal stripes—green, white, and black. The inscription "God is great" is centered on the green stripe, while another inscription, "There is no God but Allah, and Mohammed is His Prophet," is centered on the white stripe.

LOCAL ADMINISTRATION

Afghanistan is divided into provinces, districts, cities, and wards. These administrative units are led, respectively, by governors, district administrators, mayors, and heads of wards.

In each province, a provincial council and district councils are elected. Provincial councils and district councils each elect a chairperson and a secretary from among their members. The term of office for a provincial council and a district council is three years.

ECONOMY

AFGHANISTAN IS ONE of the poorest countries in the world. The Saur Revolution of 1978, the subsequent Soviet occupation, the unrelenting war waged by the *mujahedin* against the Soviets, and the civil war that followed have crippled the country's economy.

Before civil war broke out again on New Year's Day 1994, the economy appeared to be picking up. The country was taking modest steps toward rebuilding, and Kabul's marketplace was bustling with goods. Now, once again, economic development has been arrested and has taken a back seat to the war.

AGRICULTURE

Although only a little over a tenth of Afghanistan's land is arable, 70% of the population lives off the land. A large percentage of the rest of the population rears sheep or goats.

Annual rainfall is low, and farmers depend almost entirely on rivers for irrigation. Before the Soviet invasion, many ambitious schemes to harness and direct the country's rivers were underway, but most of these projects have been halted or destroyed. The Baghlan region, for example, was once richly cultivated. Today, without irrigation, much of it has been laid to waste, and the once-thriving cotton and sugar industries no longer exist. However, the Helmand canals have been restored, and fertility is returning to the land in the southwest.

Opposite: **A basket weaver in Kabul. Cottage industries help to supplement family incomes.**

Below: **Farmers winnowing grain. The Afghan economy is primarily based on agriculture.**

41

A farmer in Nangarhar. Plowing with oxen has been done for countless centuries in Afghanistan.

Another fertile region lies to the north along the boundary with the former Central Asian republics of the Soviet Union. Although agricultural products account for almost three-quarters of the national income, food crop output is barely above subsistence level.

Wheat is Afghanistan's chief crop. Sugar and cotton, in recent years, have also gained importance, providing raw material to the growing number of mills. Long before cotton mills were built, raw cotton had been an important export for Afghanistan.

Another important agricultural activity is fruit farming, which is concentrated mainly in the Kabul and Arghandab valleys. There, orchards grow apples, pears, peaches, quinces, apricots, plums, cherries, pomegranates, and many varieties of grapes and melons. Nuts, such as almonds, pistachios, and walnuts, also grow well and, together with fresh fruits and vegetables, are important exports. The main markets are India and Pakistan. Coffee is also exported.

Most of the farms in Afghanistan are small holdings farmed by individual farmers or rented out to tenants who pay their rent with part of

THE FAILURE OF THE HELMAND VALLEY PROJECT

Afghanistan's most ambitious project in the 1950s was the Helmand valley project, which attempted to harness the waters of the Helmand and its tributary, the Arghandab. The government signed a US$17 million contract with the Morrison-Knudsen Company of Idaho.

Warnings of salinity (salt content), water-logging, and the thinness of the soil were ignored. Another major drawback was the ignorance of the rural people and their opposition to modernization. The Helmand project became a white elephant that eventually cost the Afghans $55 million and another $60 million in loans and grants from the United States.

Before 1979, Afghanistan was virtually self-supporting in food, but by 1989, an estimated 33% of its agricultural land had been destroyed by the war.

their harvest. In the three decades before the Soviet invasion in 1979, an attempt by the ruling royal families to modernize the country and to bring the benefits of economic development to still medieval villages failed dismally. One of the contributing factors to the failure of the Helmand valley project was the reluctance of peasant farmers to discard their traditional methods and systems.

Today primitive farming methods are still employed. Plowing is often done with oxen and wooden plows, seeds are not scientifically selected, and land is not properly fertilized. Harvesting is performed manually; the grains are then milled by hand or sent to local mills. The farmers barter their produce for their meager needs of cloth, sugar, tea, and other basic necessities.

Livestock rearing, mostly by nomads, is the second most important occupation. The pelts, wool, skins, and meat of karakul sheep are important export commodities. Karakul wool is valued all over the world for its superior quality. The wool is popular in the United States for making superior-grade Persian-lamb coats. Other sheep are also reared for their meat, skins, and wool. Cattle provide dairy products, and1 horses, camels, and donkeys are used for transportation.

At one time much of Afghanistan was covered with forests, but these forests have almost disappeared. Most of the timber resources today are confined to the mountainous regions of Badakhshan, Wakhan, and the areas bordering Pakistan in the east.

Afghanistan's most profitable crop may well be opium from the poppies grown in the mountains near the northwest frontier provinces of Pakistan. Afghanistan and Pakistan are believed to be major producers of the drug and its main derivatives, morphine and heroin, in the Middle East and Central Asia. According to the United Nations, Afghanistan produced 2,637 tons (2,400 metric tons) of opium in 1991.

The civil war in Afghanistan has helped boost production and trafficking in the region. It was also a prime source of revenue for the *mujahedin*'s struggle against Soviet occupation in the 1980s. Much of the drug is shipped to Europe via Iran. Recently, Iran introduced several measures to curtail this trade.

HANDICRAFTS AND INDUSTRY

Many Afghans living in urban areas engage in handicrafts and trade. Every village has traditional small industries, including woodworking, leather crafting, basket weaving, pottery, tile molding, and the handmilling of grains.

Metalwork is done in small shops throughout the country using imported sheets of iron. It is in the towns that agricultural implements, such as plows, spades, pickaxes, and utensils and knives for domestic use are manufactured. Coppersmiths fashion pots, trays, and jugs—those produced in Badakhshan and Kandahar are beautifully patterned with intricate designs.

Afghanistan is also famous for its carpets. The wool and dyes are prepared locally, and the carpets are woven by hand. The best carpets can be found in Daulatabad, near Mazar-e-Sharif, and in Herat. Silk-weaving of outstanding texture is made in Herat and Nangarhar. Both cotton and wool are also handwoven.

Sheepskin coats of the best quality are made at Ghazni. Silversmiths and goldsmiths all over the country produce jewelry using centuries-old techniques.

Some small industries were started in 1920 by the government. These include tanneries, small machine-repair shops, cotton-ginning mills, bakeries, fruit processing plants, oil factories, and soap, shoe, and ceramics factories.

Larger industries include cotton, rayon, and wool mills. Afghanistan also produces its own construction material and chemical fertilizers.

MINING

Afghanistan has rich, varied, and extensive mineral resources. Its mineral deposits include chrome, copper, lead, zinc, uranium, manganese, asbestos, gold, silver, iron, sulfur, mica, nickel, slate, and salt. Lapis lazuli, amethyst, beryl, ruby, alabaster, tourmaline, jade, and quartz are just some of the precious and semiprecious gems and stones that have been discovered. Besides these, large deposits of granite, marble, gypsum, and clay for making china and soapstone have also been found.

A copper processing plant near Kabul provides 20% of the country's needs. The country's huge deposits of iron ore are largely undeveloped because of the lack of adequate infrastructure, including transportation.

Afghanistan is the world's leading producer of lapis lazuli. This deep blue semiprecious gem is obtained from the mines in the Kokcha river valley in Badakhshan and is cut and finished at the lapidarium in Kabul.

Outcrops of coal and seepages of oil and pitch occur both north and south of the Hindu Kush.

Promising layers of oil-bearing shale were first found in the north in 1936 by the American Inland Exploration Company. Additional deposits were discovered in the Arghandab valley to the west and south of Gardez. In 1954, a Swedish firm began drilling for oil in Jowzjan province and reported successful finds in 1958. It is believed that Afghanistan has some 242,000 million tons (220,000 million metric tons) of oil reserves. However, this potential has yet to be exploited, not only because of the lack of funds, but also because of the seemingly endless wars.

Natural gas exports make up as much as 42% of the country's total exports. Deposits of over 87 billion cubic yards (67 billion cubic meters) of natural gas were discovered by the Soviets at Khwaja Gogerdak and Yatim Taq, and production was started in 1967.

THE ART OF CARPET WEAVING

The art of carpet weaving is highly traditional, and the majority of patterns are jealously guarded family secrets handed down from one generation to the next. The weaving is done mostly by young girls and women, except in Turkoman, where men also weave.

The finest carpets are from Meymaneh and are woven from the wool of karakul sheep. This wool is carefully washed, carded, spun by hand, and dyed. These carpets have as many as 355 knots to the square inch (55 knots to the square centimeter), whereas a coarse carpet only has 129 to 194 knots per square inch (20 to 30 knots per square centimeter). The finest work requires four workers, who take three months to complete a rug of 6.6 square yards (six square meters).

Afghanistan has two international airports—at Kabul and Kandahar—through which tourists can enter the country. There are also about 30 local airports serving the smaller cities and towns.

TOURISM

Another source of foreign revenue, tourism, has almost completely disappeared in the last decade. In 1990, just 8,000 tourists arrived in Afghanistan, bringing receipts of about US$1 million. Some potential attractions for the foreign visitor include Bamian, with its tall statue of Buddha and thousands of painted caves, the Blue Mosque of Mazar-e-Sharif, and the mountains of the Hindu Kush.

HYDROELECTRIC POWER

In spring, melting snow from Afghanistan's mountains swells the numerous rivers and waterfalls to gushing torrents with huge potential for hydroelectric power. In the summer, when the flow is reduced to a mere trickle, dams and reservoirs are necessary to harness this power.

Hydroelectric plants have been constructed in several provinces, including Kandahar.

FOREIGN TRADE

For many years, the Soviet Union was Afghanistan's leading trading partner, often accounting for as much as half its total exports and imports. Today, Afghanistan's major trading partners include India, Pakistan, Saudi Arabia, Japan, Germany, and Britain.

Afghanistan's major imports include wheat, sugar, tea, textiles, vehicles, and petroleum products. Its principal exports are fresh and dried food, karakul sheep skins and wool, cotton, carpets and rugs, and natural gas.

PUSHTINS

Pushtins are lambskin waistcoats and overcoats with the fleece turned inward. They are embroidered, usually in the favorite color combination of blue, black, orange, and yellow.

The best pushtins are made in Ghazni. Women who live in urban areas and villages near towns embroider these and other articles of clothing, including the skullcaps worn under turbans, vests, and *burkas* ("boor-KHAHS"), a garment worn by women outdoors. Color combinations and designs vary in different parts of the country.

TRANSPORTATION

There are about 13,660 miles (22,000 kilometers) of roads in Afghanistan. All-weather highways link Kabul with Kandahar and Herat in the south and west, Jalalabad in the east, and Mazar-e-Sharif and the Amudar'ya river in the north.

In 1992, Afghanistan signed agreements with its neighbors Pakistan and Uzbekistan to construct and repair its highways. More than 2,700 miles (4,300 kilometers) of asphalt roads in Afghanistan have been destroyed since 1979.

Rivers are also an important method of transport. There are about 750 miles (1,200 kilometers) of navigable waterways in Afghanistan; the Amudar'ya is perhaps the most important. River ports on the Amudar'ya are also linked to Kabul by road.

The Jalalabad highway is one of the few major roads in Afghanistan. An improved road network is essential in the development of many sectors of the economy.

AFGHANS

THE LAST CENSUS, conducted in 1979, which was also Afghanistan's first census ever, put the country's population at slightly over 13 million. This figure, however, excluded an estimated 2.5 million nomads.

Because of the turmoil and upheaval since then, reliable statistics have been hard to obtain. To escape the civil war, millions of Afghans fled from their homes to safety in refugee camps in the neighboring countries of Pakistan and Iran.

In 1993, the population was estimated to be 21.7 million, including some three million nomads and more than six million refugees living just outside the country's borders.

Like the people of the United States, Afghans are a potpourri of ethnic and linguistic groups. This is the result of the various ethnic groups that entered Afghanistan and eventually blended with the local population, leaving their imprint on both the ethnic and cultural development of the country.

The majority of the population consists of the Mediterranean substock of the Caucasoid race, to which most of the people of the Mediterranean and Middle Eastern countries also belong. The Pushtun, Tajik, Nuristani, and Baluchi are Caucasoid.

Besides the Caucasoid, there are two other main physical types in Afghanistan—the Mongoloid and the Australoid. The Hazara, Turkmen (also known as Turkoman), Uzbek, Kirghiz, and Aimaq are Mongoloid, and the Brahui are Australoids.

Above and opposite: **Many Afghan men wear turbans tied in a way that represents affiliation to an ethnic group.**

PUSHTUNS

The Pushtuns are renowned throughout the world for their prowess on the battlefield. The most successful wars against the British in the 19th century were conducted by the Pushtuns.

The Pushtuns form about half the country's population and have traditionally been the most powerful of all the tribes in Afghanistan. They regard themselves as the true Afghans. In India and Pakistan, they are known as Pathans. As a group, they have always been synonymous with strength and fortitude.

Pushtuns appear to have lived in Afghanistan since the beginning of recorded history. Although their origin is obscure, they are believed to be of Aryan stock. Their language, Pushtu, belongs to the Indo-European group of languages and is related to Persian.

The Pushtuns have passed down a legend about their origin through the generations. They believe they owe their ancestry to Qais, who is said to have descended from King Saul and one of the lost tribes of Israel. Afghana, a son of Saul, is believed to have led his 40 sons to the hills of Ghor (now known as Hazarajat). Qais, according to Pushtun belief, was chosen by the Prophet Mohammed to spread Islam in Afghanistan.

The Pushtuns live in an area extending from the Pamirs, north of Afghanistan, across the Sulaiman range and the Helmand valley all the way to Herat and the Iranian border. They began venturing out of this mountain fastness only in the 11th century, when they joined the armies of Mahmud of Ghazni in his conquest of India. Warfare has since become an integral part of the Pushtuns' life; even today, they habitually carry firearms.

There are two main Pushtun tribes—the Ghilzais and the Durranis, who are also known as Abdalis. The Ghilzais were once nomads who moved around with their herds of cattle and sheep looking for seasonal grazing grounds. They finally settled in the area between Kandahar and the Kabul river. The Ghilzais came to prominence in the 17th century when the Abdalis were banished by the Shah of Persia.

A Pushtun warrior and his ubiquitous rifle. About seven million Pushtuns live in Pakistan, with smaller numbers in Iran and the Central Asian republics in the north.

The Ghilzais seized control of Kandahar, invaded and conquered Persia, and ruled there for a short period. In 1747, when the Durrani ruler Ahmad Shah came into power, the Ghilzais were forced to accept his rule. Traditionally the Ghilzais have always played a crucial role in the commercial and military sectors of Afghanistan.

Physically, the Pushtuns resemble true Aryan stock. They are typically tall and fair, often with aquiline features and black or brown hair and brown eyes, although hazel or even blue eyes are not uncommon.

TAJIKS

The Tajiks are of Iranian origin and, like the Pushtuns, can be divided into two principal groups. One group of Tajiks, who are Shi'ite Muslims, live mainly in the mountainous regions of Badakhshan and the Wakhan. They are farmers who live in villages that are often extremely poverty stricken.

The other group of Tajiks live around major towns like Kabul, Bamian, Herat, and in the north. They are urban dwellers and form a large part of the middle class in the larger towns. These Tajiks are Sunni Muslims and are skilled artisans and traders. Many are also farmers, and the *zaminders* ("ZAW-meen-DAHS"), or landowners, among them are accepted as leaders. Although tribal organizations no longer exist for this group, a strong communal feeling lives on.

There are some four million Tajiks in Afghanistan, about one and a half million more than in the Central Asian republic of Tajikistan itself. Another one million Tajiks live in Uzbekistan. The Tajiks are of Mediterranean stock and are generally tall with light skin and black hair, although red or even blond hair is sometimes seen. In the north, the Tajiks have more Mongoloid features.

The Tajiks are descendants of the peoples who, for centuries, defended the eastern frontiers of the Persian empire.

A Nuristani man. Nuristanis live in the few forested regions of Afghanistan and use a great deal of timber in their buildings and furniture. Their wooden houses are often two to three stories high. They thresh grains on the flat roof, keep livestock on the first floor, use the second floor for storage, and live on the top floor. Their living quarters often have elaborately carved, open verandahs.

NURISTANIS

Nuristanis are often referred to as Kafirs, or unbelievers in Islam, by other Muslim tribes because they belonged to an independent tribe until King Abdur Rahman conquered them in 1896 and converted them to Islam.

Their origins are a mystery as no artifacts or documents that would indicate their beginnings have ever been discovered. For centuries, they remained isolated, and even today, little is known about them. Their language belongs to the Dardic group and is related to the Sanskrit of northern India.

Physically, most Nuristanis resemble Mediterranean stock. They are slight of build, with light brown skin, slender noses, above-average height, and black to sometimes blond hair. Nuristanis are very conservative, place great emphasis on family ties, and are known and respected for their great physical endurance. Nuristani men traditionally wear goatskin coats and leggings over a cotton shirt, short, full cotton trousers, and soft leather boots.

A Hazara family poses for the camera, the father and elder son in their traditional skull caps. The word "hazar" is the Persian word for "one thousand," which could have referred to a division of soldiers in the Mongol army.

HAZARAS

The Hazaras live among the mountains and valleys of central Afghanistan. Hazarajat is a bare, dry region, watered by canals carefully constructed to carry as much water as possible from the few springs that are to be found.

Most of the people are shepherds who follow seasonal grazing grounds. Crop cultivation is limited because of the poor soil and lack of water. The Hazaras are hard working and frugal, but because of the adverse conditions in the region, they have been unable to prosper. Many of them have chosen to join the army, and others have been forced to seek menial labor in the cities.

Hazaras are of Mongoloid stock and are traditionally believed to be descended from the soldiers of Genghis Khan's army that swept through Afghanistan in the 13th century. Most of them are Shi'ite Muslims, unlike the majority of Afghanistan's population, who are Sunnis.

Hazara men wear skull caps and are clean shaven. The women wear long dresses instead of the baggy trousers commonly worn elsewhere in Afghanistan.

UZBEKS AND OTHER TURKISH TRIBES

North of the Hindu Kush are found the tribes descended from Central Asian Turks, or Tartars. The largest group are the Uzbeks, who number about 1.5 million. They are mostly farmers and breed animals, including horses and karakul sheep. Uzbeks have Turkish features and are usually fairer than other Afghans.

The Turkmen number about 400,000 and live along the southern bank of the Amudar'ya. The Kirghiz, who number about 35,000, are found in the narrow Wakhan strip. Both groups are nomads of Mongoloid descent.

Another Turkish tribe, the Qizil Bash, or "red heads," so-named because they wore red skull caps, were brought into Afghanistan by the Persian ruler Nadir Shah in the 18th century to garrison Kabul. Today their descendants, who are Shi'ites, occupy a separate quarter of Kabul and are employed as crafts people and clerks. Many are also traders.

A member of the Kirghiz tribe. The Kirghiz are Sunni Muslims.

To the north of Afghanistan are several nomadic tribes, such as the Kazakhs, Karlug, and Chagatai Turks. The people of these tribes speak an archaic form of Turkish and often also speak Persian. The men of the nomadic tribes wear large, soft leather boots, a belted cloak, and turbans. Clothing typical of the area is the great coat with sleeves large enough to envelope the hands and keep them warm during cold weather.

A nomad woman wears an ornamental nose ring and a headband. Nomads make up about one-seventh of Afghanistan's population.

NOMADS

As much of Afghanistan's land is barren and arid, it is not surprising that almost a quarter of the country's population is nomadic or seminomadic. The nomads roam the land, moving with the seasons, looking for grazing land for their herds.

They are fiercely conservative and abhor change. To survive the harsh environment, nomads need to be extremely hardy and tenacious, both physically and mentally. They are proud of their way of life and disdain city dwellers. The worst thing a nomadic mother can say to a disobedient daughter is, "May you marry a town dweller!"

The *powindahs* ("paw-ween-DAHS"), also known as Kachis, are the most well known of the nomads. They are Ghilzai Pushtuns who until 1961 annually migrated across the border into Pakistan in the tens of thousands, their camels and donkeys laden with everything they owned or needed, from their tents to their babies.

Once across the border, they sold their wares, such as wool and hides. On their return trip, they brought back goods for their own consumption or to sell in Afghanistan. The *powindahs* traveled at night and camped during the day. This cycle of migration went on for centuries until interrupted by a border dispute with Pakistan in 1961.

The *powindah* men are tall, with piercing eyes and large moustaches. They wear large turbans and are invariably armed with a dagger and rifle.

The women wear colorful long-sleeved dresses over trousers and cover their heads with long shawls. They also often wear heavy silver bracelets on their wrists and ankles and other ornaments. These accessories make them look very similar to the Gypsies who roam the length and breadth of Europe. The women's bright clothes and ornaments seem to compensate for the dull, colorless landscape in which they live.

OTHERS

There are many groups of Afghans who call themselves *sayyid* ("suh-YEED") and claim Arab descent. They speak a form of Arabic. Several thousand Jews also live in the major towns and are merchants, traders, and moneylenders. Many went to Israel but eventually returned.

Thousands of Hindus and Sikhs from the Indian subcontinent have also settled in Afghanistan and can be found mainly in the towns. Most have become Afghan citizens.

The Brahui, who are found in southwestern Afghanistan, are, like the people of southern India, Dravidians, and little is known about how they arrived here and in Pakistan. In Afghanistan, many work as tenant farmers for Baluchi landlords.

THE MINGLING OF AFGHAN BLOOD

Except for some of the Pushtun areas in the south and the east of the country, few Afghans are of a single ethnic descent. Over the centuries, there has been much intermarriage among the different groups in contact with each other in the same regions.

In the north, among the Tajiks and the Uzbeks, a surprising mixture of Caucasoid and Mongoloid features is often found. Red or blond hair and blue eyes are sometimes seen with epicanthic fold and high cheekbones. Similarly, blue- or green-eyed Baluchis and Brahui, who are normally dark-skinned, are not uncommon.

LIFESTYLE

THE UNWRITTEN LAWS AND CODES of *Pushtunwalli* ("PUHSH-toon-WAH-lee") reign supreme in Afghanistan. Although basically belonging to the Pushtuns, *Pushtunwalli* is recognized and upheld by all Afghans.

Self-pride and tribal and family honor come above all else. Life is taken or sacrificed at the slightest hint of insult or loss of honor. Nor are injustices to self or family or even tribe easily forgotten or forgiven. Thus feuds can sometimes go on for generations.

Afghan society is a patriarchal one. The son brings his bride to the ancestral home, and

Above: **A village local council in session. Minor disputes, such as theft and trespass, may be dealt with during these meetings.**

Opposite: **A Pushtun villager milking a goat. Some 44,000 tons (40,000 metric tons) of goats' milk are produced in Afghanistan every year.**

often several generations live together, either in one home or nearby in the same village. Even when Afghans migrate to the towns and cities or move to other villages, family members still get together for important events, and an avid interest is taken in everyone else's affairs.

Every family is headed by a patriarch, and the tribes are, in turn, led by the *khan* ("KHAN"). All important judgements and decisions are made by the local council, or *jirgah* ("jorhr-GAH"). Everyone has a right to voice an opinion, but the final decision made by the *jirgah* must be adhered to without exception. Besides heading the decision-making and the passing of judgment, the *khan* is also responsible for the safety and prosperity of his village and must be a person with qualities of moral strength, wisdom, piety, bravery, and hospitality. He must also be of impeccable ancestry.

The *Pushtunwalli* covers a large area of human behavior, the most important being honor, revenge, and hospitality. Every child is indoctrinated by its principles from birth. Any breach can be severely punished, with anything from ostracism and exile to death.

The Pushtunwalli *decrees that guests, whether friend or foe, must be provided for and honored. A traveler in Afghanistan never lacks food or shelter.*

To the Afghan, nothing is as despicable as cowardice, and personal or family honor, *ghayrat* ("gheh-RAHT"), must be upheld at all cost. Promises made, no matter what the circumstances, must always be kept.

Fierce family and tribal affiliation leads to the Afghan belief in the right to raid other tribes to take food and provisions for their own. This is also a harsh country, and the availability of water is all-important; the tribes have to compete for what little is available. Life is devoid of any but the most basic material necessities, and a sense of pride and belonging makes life worth living. Thus the Afghan is a fighter, battling against the hard conditions of his or her lot.

Much of this way of life is left behind when the villager moves to the towns and cities. Society is no longer classless; the educated and the rich form the upper crust of society. The professionals, teachers, and government and industrial employees make up the bulk of the growing middle class. Back home in the villages, the old are revered, and their advice is sought and always followed. In urban Afghanistan, this is no longer true, and the elderly feel unwanted and lost. Many seek solace in hashish and other drugs.

THE CODES OF *PUSHTUNWALLI*

- To avenge blood; to fight to the death for anyone who has taken refuge with one; to defend to the last any property entrusted to one.
- To be hospitable and safeguard the person and property of a guest.
- Not to kill a woman, a Hindu, a minstrel, or a boy not as yet circumcised.
- To pardon any wrong, with the exception of murder, at the intercession of a woman, the wrongdoer's family member, a *sayyid*, or a *mullah*. To punish adultery with death.
- To spare anyone who takes sanctuary in a mosque or shrine. Also to spare in battle anyone who begs for mercy.

LIFE IN THE VILLAGES

The villages in Afghanistan are clustered around the larger towns and cities in a nuclear pattern. The houses are flat roofed and built with bricks and plastered with a mixture of mud and straw. In the west, along the border with Iran, and in the northern plains, are found square, domed roofs, and in the south, the nomadic and seminomadic tribes build semicircular, beehive-shaped reed huts.

Most houses have an enclosed compound that shelters the livestock and holds sheds for storage. Here too are found the cooking area and the general living area where the family works and plays.

The women walk to the nearest stream or pool to collect water, to bathe, and to do the laundry. Some of the more affluent households have their own artificially made pools or streams, called *juy* ("joo-YEE"). The trips to the streams provide the women with a chance to get away from home for a while and to socialize with each other.

A typical village in Afghanistan, with mud and brick houses. The vast majority of Afghans live in rural areas.

Arab geographers first wrote about the windmills of Herat in the seventh century. The entire region of what was known in ancient times as Khorason, along the border with Iran, was covered with windmills, and ruins of windmills were also found in the south, stretching from Kabul and Ghazni to the Indus river. Some historians believe the windmills in Europe and China were inspired by them.

Some sort of accommodation is always provided for travelers in the villages, and where circumstances permit, carpeted rooms are kept to entertain guests in the home. The mosques double up as schools and often also provide meeting places for the local *jirgahs*. In some villages, however, communal affairs are conducted under shady trees.

Household furnishing is simple, consisting of cooking utensils, basic dishes, and some heirlooms, such as religious mementoes, weapons, brass or copper utensils, and storage chests and containers. Large earthenware pots are used to store grains. Some villagers possess string beds, but most sleep on mattresses, which are laid out on the floor at night and neatly stacked in a corner during the day.

The flat roofs are used in summer for sleeping and for drying fruits and vegetables. An earthen platform is often built in front of the house for the same purpose. In summer, the food is cooked outdoors. Charcoal and dung patties, together with roots and branches, are used for fuel. The dung patties are made by the women and children, who collect the manure, form them into patties, and slap them on the walls and rocks to dry.

Mud and brick structures that look like block houses, with rectangular holes for circulation of the air, are built to dry grapes to make raisins. Windmills are found in Herat, but they only operate during the "time of the 120 days' wind," between June and September.

The Afghans have invented a simple but ingenious system of keeping themselves warm. In the villages south of the Hindu Kush, houses have hot-air tunnels, or *tawkhanah* ("teh-KHAH-nah"), built under the floor, and a fire at one end warms up the whole floor. In other places, a small, low table is placed over a charcoal brazier, and a blanket is spread over this table to contain the heat. The family sits around the table to keep warm. This unique system is called *sandali* ("sehn-dah-LEE").

NOMADIC LIFE

The nomads follow their herds to summer and winter grazing grounds. The seminomads move in summer to pastures with their herds and return in winter to tend crops on their farms. The nomads provide several services to the villagers. Besides supplying animal products, they form lines of communication between the different regions. The animal dung left when they pass over the fields helps to fertilize the land. Often they act as moneylenders, lending money to the farmers.

Their tents are built with or without frames. The nomads build their frameless tents with black goats' hair, and these come in three major styles: the south and western Durrani Pushtun tent; the eastern and northern Ghilzai tent; and the barrel-vaulted tent found in Baluchistan. A fourth style of frameless tent, *arabi* ("erh-rah-BEE"), is found among the Aimaq.

The seminomads live in *yurts* ("yerhts"), tents with a portable lattice-like framework. The frame is covered with reeds and a number of colored, woven bands. A series of long poles tied with special knots support the pole at the top of the wood-framed foundation.

The nomads favor tents that can easily be put up or dismantled. The tents are woven from goats' hair, which is considerably more durable than sheep's wool.

The poles are curved to fit into a slotted, hollow wooden disc at the top of the *yurt*. Felt, often elaborately decorated, is tied over the top of the tent, with the design on the inside. The door is made of carved wood.

Nomadic migration resembles a military operation. The younger shepherds move along the higher trails with the sheep and goats, while the older people and children move along lower valley trails with the other animals. They may travel 3–15 miles (5–24 kilometers) in a day, and when they stop for the night, the men settle the animals for the night and stand guard. The rest of the work is done by the women; they put up and dismantle the tents, load and unload the animals, do the housework, and prepare the food.

A camel caravan crosses the southern plains of Afghanistan. Many nomads in recent times have purchased or hired trucks to carry their luggage and the women and children.

URBAN AFGHANISTAN

Towns in Afghanistan are usually situated at the intersection of major trails or near the larger rivers. Since 1953, asphalt roads have been built around most towns. The towns act as commercial, administrative, and communication centers for the surrounding villages.

Agricultural produce, handicrafts, and raw materials are brought here by the villagers to be sent to the cities. Transport within the towns is usually by horse cart. Civil servants, who are involved in the administration of the surrounding villages, and landlords who own land in the villages generally prefer to live in the towns.

Finished goods from the cities are transported by truck to the towns. There, they are sold in the bazaar or main street of the town; most shop owners live above their shops. Besides these shops, various kinds of artisans providing services needed by the villagers can also be found in the bazaars.

One of the brightly painted trucks often found on Afghanistan's roads, transporting goods between towns and villages. In 1990, there were about 25,000 commercial vehicles in use in the country.

Shopkeepers in Kabul awaiting customers. Much of the sugar, tea, cigarettes, and soap that Afghans consume are imported from other countries.

Caravanserais ("korh-VOHN-seh-ROI"), or inns, and teahouses are found in the towns. The latter are to the Afghans what bars are to Americans. Here, the men gather to smoke water pipes, drink strongly brewed tea, and exchange the latest news. The Muslim prohibition against alcohol is almost universally observed.

The teahouses are also known as *chaykhanas* ("chaw-KHAH-nahs"). Unlike in the past, when news was spread solely by word of mouth, nowadays all *chaykhanas* have radios. News is heard and discussed, and patrons listen to music and songs from Indian movies. Afghanistan has no home-grown movie industry. Indian movies are very popular throughout the country, and there are theaters in all the major towns and cities.

Cities have sprung up where major routes meet and provide access to the outside world. The five main cities of Afghanistan are Kabul, Kandahar, Herat, Mazar-e-Sharif, all with populations of over 100,000, and Kunduz. Kabul is by far the largest city in Afghanistan, with an estimated two million residents in 1994.

Just as in the towns, there are bazaars in the cities, on appropriately larger scales. The Kabul bazaar is one of the busiest markets in Central Asia. Here, almost every kind of merchandise imaginable is sold in its own special section. Goods produced on a small scale by individuals and on a much larger scale by factories are either exported or sold locally in the bazaars.

Many people are migrating from the rural areas to the cities in search of employment. This migration increases when work on the farms ceases. Some stay temporarily and later move back to the countryside; others settle in the cities permanently.

Many Hazaras have moved to Kabul. Some became self-employed, trading in wood products, butter, and lard, or making aluminum pots and pans. Most work as laborers, gathering at specific spots every morning for foremen to recruit them. Many Tajiks also go to cities to work as drivers. After saving enough money, they buy either land or their own trucks.

High-rise buildings are common in the cities, especially Kabul, where construction has spread the city limits in all directions. Most structures in towns are built with bricks baked in kilns. Recently, however, progress in the building industry has been halted and much has been destroyed in the recent civil war. An infrastructure of restaurants, supermarkets, stores, and garages cater to the needs of the growing middle class and the foreigners who remain. Facilities in the cities, though significantly better than in rural areas, still have much room for improvement, particularly in the area of plumbing and water supply.

Life in the cities is constantly changing, as Afghans are quickly adapting to modern ideas. Changes in the smaller towns take place more gradually. In the rural areas, living patterns are almost at a standstill, and people live as they have done for hundreds of years.

According to UNESCO, there were some 1,745,000 radio receivers and 135,000 television sets in Afghanistan in 1990.

ROLE OF WOMEN IN AFGHANISTAN

Women in Afghanistan are required to observe the *purdah*. They must cover themselves so as not to be seen by any men other than those immediately related to them. Traditional Afghan women wear the *chadri* ("CHAW-dree"), a voluminous garment with only a slit or net for the eyes, over their normal clothes whenever they go outdoors.

Women in Afghanistan have traditionally held secondary roles in society. They must obey their husbands or fathers and seek their permission in almost everything they do. Nevertheless, women are far from being weak; they wield much power in their own homes, where they reign supreme as home-makers. They also have considerable influence over the decisions made by the men.

The women of rural Afghanistan are physically strong and can work just as hard as the men. They are reputed to be courageous and well able to face the dangers of their environment. Most of them have learned to handle firearms and to use them for protection against robbers and wild animals.

In marriage and divorce, Afghanistan follows Islamic laws. A man only needs to repeat "I divorce you" three times in front of a witness to divorce his wife. A woman, on the other hand, has to appear before a judge with reasons for a divorce. Simple though it may sound, divorce is not common. A great deal of social stigma is attached to divorce. Also, the requirement to pay alimony as well as the difficulty in replacing a wife, who plays an important role in the management of the home, the land, and livestock, make divorce unattractive to most men. Polygamy is permitted in Islam, and a man is allowed to take up to four wives, a practice that is not very common in Afghanistan. Adultery is punishable by death, according to Islamic laws.

Property is usually divided among the sons, the daughters having received their share as dowry. Widows are provided for—a widow receives one-eighth of her husband's property and the assurance of a home and protection by his family. She also controls the jewelry, passing it on to her daughters or daughters-in-law, as she likes.

Women in rural Afghanistan enjoy greater freedom than their sisters in the towns in not having to wear the *chadri*. The need for them to work side by side with their men in the fields frees them from wearing cumbersome clothes. However, they have to keep their distance from other men. The women of the nomadic tribes move freely, going about their daily affairs unrestricted by rules of gender segregation.

King Amanullah, in the 1920s, tried to emancipate women by encouraging coeducation, removing the veil requirement, and promoting the use of Western dress. This angered the religious and conservative elements of Afghan society and led to his eventual downfall. During the years of Soviet occupation, many women in the larger cities, especially Kabul, where European influence is most strongly felt, took to wearing Western dress. The vigorous efforts of the communist government to improve the status of women was one reason for widespread rebellion by conservative Afghans. Despite disapproval from conservative Afghans, many urban Afghan women have ventured to work outside their homes since 1959. They constitute a growing percentage of the work force in towns, particularly in health services and education. Female participation in government is, however, minuscule.

According to the 1979 population census, women made up less than 8% of the surveyed work force, numbering just 300,000 out of a total of 3,900,000 workers.

Opposite: **A *chadri*-clad woman. In the countryside, where the *chadri* is not worn, women cover their faces at the sight of an unknown person.**

A father and his son in Paktia province. Families will always take care of their relatives, whatever their own difficulties.

FAMILY RELATIONSHIPS

Families in Afghanistan are close-knit, and a strong sense of responsibility exists toward all members of the nuclear as well as the extended family. The extended family often includes all those who can trace descent from a common ancestor. Similarly, kinship includes those whose ancestors were brothers.

As is the norm in most Islamic societies, there are no family names, and recognition is given by reference to the fathers. In spite of this, the original family of most Afghans is known by all. Any disgrace or honor earned by an individual is felt by all those who claim kinship.

Relationships are also given due distinction. Paternal uncles are called *kaka* ("kaw-kaw") and maternal uncles *mama* ("maw-maw"). Every relationship is thus well defined and recognized.

Another important aspect of Afghan family relationships is the order of birth. Upon the death of the father, the eldest brother, by virtue of his birth rank, becomes the most powerful in the family and receives a larger share of the inheritance.

In the urban areas, where Western culture has greater influence, the family unit often consists only of the nuclear family. When a son marries, he stays with his parents only a short while before moving out to his own home with his bride. The size of the family can often depend on the financial position of the family, which determines whether another home can be afforded.

MARRIAGE

In many Afghan stories and folklore, marriage is based on romance. In real life, however, most marriages are arranged by the parents and the relatives. There is a strict moral code, and chastity is prescribed for unmarried men and women.

Marriages are often arranged when the couple are still children. A man does not marry until he is 18–20, or a woman until she is 16–18. Marriages between cousins, especially paternal ones, are greatly favored as they are seen to increase the already strong family ties.

In marriages within a family, the bride-price, which can often be steep, is forfeited. The bride-price is paid by the groom's family to compensate for the loss of a valuable family member. The dowry is paid by the bride's family—this consists of household goods, which in the urban society include electrical goods and other modern gadgets.

When the parents decide that their children are ready for marriage, a relative is sought to act as go-between. He or she handles the financial negotiations, which may last for months. In some segments of modern society, the services of the go-between are often dispensed with, and the families enter into direct negotiations.

In the past, if a girl died after the engagement, her family would replace her with another girl in the family. If the husband died after marriage, a brother of the husband would take the widow as his wife. This custom is no longer popular.

WIFE-STEALING IN AFGHANISTAN

In Turkoman, the bride is "captured" from her father's *yurt* by the groom's friends and kinsmen. The "marauders" are attacked by the bride's family and friends, who throw eggs at them.

Even as late as the 19th century, wife stealing was popular in this region of Afghanistan. If a boy and girl eloped, the families had to accept them, fix the dowry and the bride-price, and hold the appropriate ceremonies for the marriage. In the rest of Afghanistan, this practice would have brought disgrace to the families.

A law was passed in 1950 to curtail the spending of enormous sums on lavish wedding, birth, and death ceremonies. The law has mostly been ignored.

Occasionally, the man and woman are involved in the choice of a marriage partner, but parental approval is still required. Once the negotiations are complete, several women from the groom's family go to the bride's house for the promising ceremony. They are served tea and given sweets. Within a week, the tray in which the sweets were presented to them is sent by the groom's family, filled with money, and the engagement is announced. Wedding gifts, consisting of jewelry and clothing, are delivered by women from the groom's family before the wedding.

The wedding lasts for three days, and most of the expenses are borne by the groom's family. The bride's entourage goes to the groom's home on the first day to socialize and to get to know his family. The next day, the groom leads a procession on a horse, with musicians and dancers, to announce his arrival. Rifles are fired at intervals during the procession. The festivities continue on the third day with a feast, singing, and dancing at the groom's house; various games are played while the guests banter with the groom. In the evening, the procession picks up the bride from the bride's home and winds back to the groom's house; this time the bride rides in front of the groom on horseback.

The official ceremony, the *nikah-namah* ("ni-KAH-naw-MAH") takes place on the third night. The *nikah-namah* is the signing of the marriage contract before witnesses. This ceremony ends with recitations from the Koran by the officiating *mullah* and the throwing of sugared almonds and walnuts on the bridegroom.

In the cities, the more Westernized Afghans no longer hold such long and elaborate weddings. They combine all the ceremonies so the wedding lasts for only a day, with all the rituals usually occurring at one of the popular restaurants. Most of the guests and even the groom wear Western dress; the bride is still likely to wear a traditional green or red velvet dress.

CHILDREN

A midwife is always available, even among the nomads, to assist the mother at childbirth. There is a great deal of rejoicing, especially if the baby is a boy. The celebrations may go on for as long as three days, with guns being fired, drums beaten, and food distributed to the poor.

On the third day, the baby is given its name, usually chosen by its paternal uncles. Among the more urbanized families, the parents choose the name. The *mullah* first whispers "Allah-u-Akbar" (God is great) in the baby's ear and then whispers its name. He also informs the baby about its ancestry and exhorts it to be a good Muslim and to uphold its family's honor.

Among the nomads, the paternal uncle gives the child its name and assumes a role similar to that of a godfather in Christian societies. He will be responsible for the child if the father dies.

The birth of a boy has greater significance because he will be an heir, and because he will be indoctrinated from a young age with the principles of *Pushtunwalli* and expected to uphold the good name and honor of his family. Girls are not ill treated, but their needs always come second to those of the males in the family, and they may even be neglected. All the children are brought up in the women's quarters. The mother breastfeeds the child until the next baby comes or the child is too old.

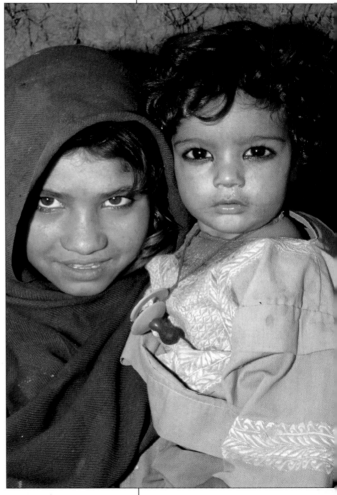

Girls look after younger siblings, and by age 10 they are expected to have the skills of a homemaker.

In the cities, the baby's birth is celebrated on the seventh day. It is at this celebration that the baby is named. The guests arrive bearing gifts for the newborn, and there is singing and dancing in the women's quarters.

Weaning is often sudden, and so is transition into adulthood. The children are toilet trained by their mothers when still very young and taught to feed themselves. It is the mother who must discipline the children; their fathers usually indulge them. However, it is the father who usually bathes and dresses his little sons.

The women in Afghanistan wield power in family affairs, and the participation of men in some family duties is seen as an example of women's influence. Men who are favored by the women of a household also have greater say in domestic matters.

In rural societies, young boys learn to watch over the animals as they graze. Unlike Western society, there is no marked adolescence. When a boy is about 7 years old, he is circumcised, usually by an itinerant barber.

A feast is held, with games of physical skill and prizes of money or expensive turban cloth given to the victors by the father. After this, the boy is treated as a man; he is allowed to wear a turban or cap and is expected to take care of himself. He must begin to help his father in the fields. A nomad child learns to ride and shoot, and watches the herds.

No ceremony marks a girl's arrival at puberty, but in certain areas, especially Paktia, molasses is distributed among the women. The girls help to look after their younger siblings and, like the boys, watch over the grazing herds. By the time they are about 9 or 10, they learn all the skills to be a good mother and wife. They are able to grind wheat and corn, fetch water, cook, sew, clean, and make dung patties for fuel.

Afghanistan has one of the highest infant mortality rates in the world. From statistics given by Save the Children Fund, an estimated 123 out of every 1,000 children die before they are a year old, and 226 die before their fifth birthday.

EDUCATION

Until the early 1900s, the only education available was at mosque schools, which were attended only by the boys. The girls acquired their religious training from elderly women, who conducted classes at home.

King Habibullah founded the first modern school in Kabul in 1903. He refuted opposition from the *mullahs* with the argument that providing an education was deemed an obligation by the Prophet Mohammed. He patterned the school on the Aligarh University in India and called it Habibia. Secular as well as Islamic subjects were taught. By World War I, foreign teachers had been added to the staff.

King Habibullah also founded a military academy for army officers and a training college for teachers. Education made further rapid strides under the reign of King Habibullah's successor, King Amanullah, when a number of schools were opened in urban as well as some rural areas.

A teacher conducts a class in an open-air village school. Primary education, which is officially compulsory, begins at age 7 and lasts for eight years.

77

Since 1979, higher education has been disrupted by the departure of much of the teaching staff from Afghanistan. In the late 1980s, more than 15,000 Afghan students were sent to colleges and institutes in the Soviet Union and eastern Europe.

Habibia had by then become an academic high school patterned on the French secondary school, and its first high school class graduated in 1923. Four more high schools were opened in Kabul and other major towns between 1923 and 1928. The first school for girls was opened in Kabul in 1924. The constitution of 1931 made primary education compulsory and free for all children. However, by 1940 there were still only 250 primary schools for boys, and even by 1967, the government had not succeeded in providing adequate facilities.

After World War II, Afghanistan's educational system was greatly influenced by the United States, Britain, France, and Germany. During the 1950s, more girls' schools were opened in spite of opposition from conservative Afghans. Progress in education was often slow because of poor attendance. In the rural areas, parents were reluctant to forgo their children's help in the fields, and many children could not attend school for several months during the winter. Moreover, educating the children of nomads was difficult. Mobile schools, whose teachers followed the tribes, were introduced to address this problem.

Village schools are often run by a single person and modeled on the mosque schools. The different languages spoken present a major problem, and the official language of the school is the first language of the majority in the region. The Koran, however, is taught in Arabic.

By 1967, there were some 58 vocational schools offering courses in agriculture, technology, commerce, economics, arts and crafts, tailoring, secretarial services, and home economics. In addition, there were special training programs in civil aviation, community development, accountancy and finance, radio operation, and nursing.

Higher education began in 1932 with the founding of the faculty of medicine. This was followed in the 1940s by the faculties of law, science,

and literature. In 1946, the University of Kabul was founded. Originally, as a concession to the conservative segments of society, separate faculties of medicine, science, and letters were run for women. By 1960, all faculties were coeducational.

Education has become increasingly important to the urban population, and acquiring a foreign education is considered very prestigious. As with everything else in Afghanistan, war has set back education, with an entire generation of children languishing in refugee camps in Iran and Pakistan.

During the Soviet occupation, of the 1.57 million children in refugee camps who were of school-going age, no more than 20% received formal education of any kind. Higher and secondary education was even more badly affected, with only about 145 high schools for hundreds of thousands of students. With only 78 primary schools for girls, education for girls was negligible. There remained a great deal of prejudice against educating girls. Most schools in the refugee camps were run by Christian organizations, and their influence was feared by the parents.

Kirghiz children read their books inside a *yurt*. The total enrollment at primary and secondary schools, as a proportion of the school-age population, dropped from 29% in 1981 to only 19% in 1989.

DEATH

When a Muslim is on his or her deathbed, family and friends gather around to recite verses from the Koran and lament. Often this can be very loud and dramatic, even though Islam advocates the acceptance of death as an act of Allah.

Once a man dies, his male relations, with the help of the *mullah* who recites the prayers, bathe the body. Female relations do this for a deceased woman. The ritual ablution, which is normally performed before the daily prayers, is performed on the body. The body is then shrouded in white cloth, and the toes are tied together.

The body must be buried as soon as possible, but never at night. It is taken to the mosque, where a prayer for the dead is said in Arabic. In urban Afghanistan, the body remains at home while a prayer service is held at the mosque. Occasionally this prayer is held at the graveside.

The grave must be six feet (1.8 meters) long and at least two feet (0.6 meter) deep to allow the corpse to sit up on the Day of Judgment. The feet must point toward Mecca, so that when the corpse sits up, it will face Mecca. In some areas, the body is buried on its right side, with the face toward Mecca.

Pottery or stone lamps are lighted on the grave, and for a year, prayers are held for the deceased every Thursday night. On the 14th and 40th days, close relatives and friends visit first the grave, to offer prayers, then the deceased's home, where the family will have prepared a meal. The same ritual is held after a year. On the anniversary of the death, the women of the family, who have worn only white for that period, visit the grave to be released from mourning.

Many rituals and beliefs are a throwback to the practices of pre-Islamic times. Head and foot markers on graves in Nuristan look very much like grave effigies from Kafir, or pre-Islamic, times. In Pushtun areas, a narrow white cloth is tied from the head to the foot of a grave. When this strip breaks, it is believed that the soul has escaped to purgatory to await the Day of Judgment. It is also believed that the damned soul of an improperly buried person can return to kill and enslave other souls and can be controlled only by practitioners of black magic. Afghans never remove any plant from a graveyard, for this is believed to bring death to the family or release an evil spirit who may be imprisoned in the roots.

RELIGION

TOGETHER WITH Buddhism and Christianity, Islam is one of the three major religions of the world. Although the Middle East has traditionally been the stronghold of Islam, the religion also has hundreds of millions of adherents throughout the rest of the world, with sizable populations in countries such as Pakistan, India, China, Indonesia, Malaysia, and the United States, where some five million Muslims live.

Islam was founded by the Prophet Mohammed in Mecca in the seventh century. Mohammed, according to tradition, received revelations from Allah through the Angel Gabriel when he was about 40 years old. These revelations were compiled and written in the Koran and form the basis for the tenets of Islam.

Afghanistan has been an Islamic state since 1992 when the various *mujahedin* groups succeeded in overthrowing the Soviet-backed President Rabbani. Over 90% of the population are Muslim. Most Afghans are Sunni Muslims, and the remainder, mostly Hazara, are Shi'ite Muslims.

Islam forms an extremely strong bond among the diverse tribes and peoples of this country. Their strong faith in their religion spurred the Afghans to withstand the Soviet onslaught. The tenets and beliefs of Islam guide its adherents in any given situation, whether personal, social, economic, or political.

Islam not only dictates the religious observances and rituals pertaining to the religion but also lays down laws for almost all aspects of everyday life. Because of this, the *mullahs* held extensive power over much of the Afghan lifestyle for centuries.

The increase in secular education and greater urbanization in the 20th century have eroded some of the *mullahs'* influence. However, with the *mujahedin* groups now in power, Islam can be expected to take on a even greater role in the Afghan's life.

In the eighth century, all of the Prophet Mohammed's known sayings, decisions, and responses to life situations and to philosophical and legal questions were brought together in a book called the Sunna *("SOON-nah"). This collection, together with the Koran, forms the source for the Islamic faith and legal system.*

Opposite: **The Blue Mosque of Mazar-e-Sharif is one of hundreds of mosques in Afghanistan. Mosques are typically decorated with floral or calligraphic designs.**

THE FIVE PILLARS OF ISLAM

Islam imposes five main obligations on its followers. These laws are written down in the Koran, the basic source of Islamic teachings.

SHAHADAT The most important principle of Islam is the belief that Allah is the one and only God and Mohammed is His prophet or messenger. This, the first pillar of Islam, is called the *shahadat* ("sheh-hah-DEHT"). Anyone who converts to Islam must take an oath that on the Day of Judgment he or she will bear witness to this belief.

SALAT ("saw-LAWT"), or prayers, is the second pillar. After ritual ablutions, a Muslim must pray five times a day, facing toward Mecca, Islam's holy city. The prayers must be said at dawn, immediately after noon, in the late afternoon, at dusk, and at night.

The faithful are called to these prayers by the *muezzin* ("moo-EZ-in"), using the call to prayer known as the *azan* ("eh-ZAHN"). The prayer may be performed by the individual alone or with the congregation in a mosque. Praying in a mosque is more usual for Muslim men than women, and women who go to the mosque must pray in an area set aside for them. Friday is the Muslim Sabbath, when all must gather for the noon prayer at the mosque, and a sermon is delivered by the religious leader of that community or by an Islamic scholar.

ZAKAT Every Muslim must give a certain percentage of personal wealth to the poor every year. This is usually done in the month of Ramadan, when Muslims fast. The payment, or *zakat* ("zeh-KAHT"), can be made directly or indirectly, through the clergy or the government. In Afghanistan, the traditional amount is two and a half percent. This act is said to purify a Muslim's possessions.

SAWM During the month of Ramadan, the ninth month of the Muslim calendar, no food or drink can be consumed between dawn and dusk. The act of fasting is called *sawm* ("SAWM"). The dawn meal, called *sahari* ("seh-heh-REE"), is eaten to sustain the individual until dusk, when the fast is broken with the evening meal, known as *iftar* ("eef-TAHR").

In most towns and villages, these times are announced from the mosque. In Kabul, the cannon on Sher Darwaza Hill is fired an hour before sunrise so that people can wake up and eat. The second time the cannon is fired, all eating must cease. At dusk, the cannon is again fired to announce the end of the fasting.

HAJJ The *hajj* ("HAHJ") is the pilgrimage to Mecca in Saudi Arabia, where the Ka'bah, believed by Muslims to be the House of Allah on earth, was built by Abraham at Allah's command. On the ninth day of the 12th month of the Islamic calendar, the pilgrim must perform set rituals and prayers at the Ka'bah and in strategic places in its vicinity. The next day, animals are slaughtered, as a sacrifice to Allah and to commemorate the slaying of a sheep by Abraham, in place of his son Isaac, at Allah's command.

It is the duty of every Muslim to visit the holy city of Mecca in Saudi Arabia at least once in their lives, unless prevented from doing so by reason of poverty or illness.

Opposite: **Kirghiz children learn to read the Koran. As the Koran is in Arabic, learning the language is a prerequisite. Many educated Muslims memorize passages from the Koran, making it a lifelong task. The meanings of passages that refer to rituals and living guidelines have to be interpreted and understood and not simply memorized.**

There are similarities and differences between the Koran and the Bible. The Koran recognizes a line of prophets, including Moses and the prophets of the Old Testament, but Muslims believe Mohammed is the last in the line. Like the Bible, the Koran affirms the existence of angels as God's messengers, but it also mentions the jinns, spiritual beings created from fire. Rebellious jinns are called demons, and Satan is believed to be the chief demon.

SHI'ITES AND SUNNIS

After the death of the Prophet Mohammed in 632, his followers split into two groups when there was disagreement over his successor. The Sunnis were those who believed that his successor should be elected from among the Prophet's companions. The Shi'ites were those who believed that the Prophet had appointed his son-in-law and cousin, Ali, as his successor. Over the centuries, other differences between the Sunnis and Shi'ites evolved, but the original dispute over the succession to Prophet Mohammed remains the most crucial of the differences.

Today, more than 90% of the world's estimated one billion Muslims are Sunnis. Afghanistan's neighbor Iran and Iraq have Shi'ite majorities. Most Afghans, about 80% of the population, are Sunnis. The Shi'ite minority is made up of the Hazaras, the Qizil Bash, and many Tajiks. The Ismailee Muslims, whose faith is an offshoot of the Shi'ites, are also found among the mountain Tajiks. Afghans believe that Ali is buried in Mazar-e-Sharif.

PRE-ISLAMIC BELIEFS

The religious beliefs of rural Afghan Muslims are still mixed with the superstitions and rituals of their pre-Islamic past. Most villagers believe in the influence of good and bad spirits and try to placate them. Jinns, mentioned in the Koran as spiritual beings, are thought to threaten women and children with evil. Amulets and talismans are acquired and worn for protection.

There are numerous shrines, or tombs of saintly persons, in Afghanistan. Women, especially, go to these to receive blessings or to ask for special favors. To make a wish or to swear vengeance, a piece of colored cloth is tied to a stick buried near the shrine.

THE *JIHAD*

Sometimes referred to as the sixth pillar of Islam, the *jihad* ("jee-HAHD") is, in theory, the permanent struggle to make the word of Allah supreme. The Koran advocates the sword only as a last resort. Disbelievers, according to some passages in the Koran, should be guaranteed the freedom to practice their own religion under Islamic rule.

The concept of the *jihad* has been abused by unscrupulous Muslims throughout history. To the Afghans constantly involved with war, however, the *jihad* has taken on great meaning. Throughout the years of the Soviet occupation, the *jihad* was the main driving force of the Afghan *mujahedin*. Those killed in the confrontation with the communists were called *shuhada* ("shoo-hah-DAH"), or martyrs, and buried in a martyrs' cemetery (shown here).

For some Muslims, the *jihad* can also be interpreted as a sacred struggle against any enemy, real or abstract, such as poverty and other social illnesses, that may impede the progress of an Islamic society.

According to the Koran, those who died in the cause of the jihad *are guaranteed a place in heaven.*

NON-MUSLIMS

Non-Muslims make up a very small portion of Afghanistan's population—just 1%. They are predominantly urban dwellers. Despite their small numbers, the Sikhs, Hindus, and Jews have played a leading role in the country's commercial life.

A small community of Parsis, who are Zoroastrians, has remained in Afghanistan. But of the other older religions that, in ancient times, had strong connections with Afghanistan, nothing remains.

LANGUAGE

AFGHANISTAN'S MANY ETHNIC GROUPS speak a great variety of languages. The two most important languages are Pushtu, the language of the Pushtuns, the largest group in the country, and Dari, a language similar to Persian. Both Pushtu and Dari are official languages in Afghanistan and most Afghans will understand at least one or the other.

Many of Afghanistan's languages, including Pushtu and Dari, have a common root because over 10 million Afghans speak languages of the Indo-European language family. Among them are the Pushtuns, Tajiks, Hazaras, Aimaq tribes, Baluchis, and Nuristanis. The other major language family in Afghanistan is Turkic, which is spoken by the Uzbeks, Turkomans, Kirghiz, and other Turkish tribes. Turkic languages predominate in the northern regions.

THE INDO-EUROPEAN LANGUAGES

The Indo-European group of languages includes the languages of Iran, India, and Pakistan. Scholars believe that the Indo-European languages were brought to these countries by Aryan invaders about 3,000 years ago. All the different languages of the Indo-European family have the same structure, and many of the words in their vocabularies sound similar as they stem from the same linguistic matrix.

Most Pushtuns speak Pushtu. The Tajiks and some of the urban Pushtuns speak Dari. The Hazaras use Hazaragi, which is a dialect of Dari. The distribution of dialects and languages forms a pattern related to the different geographical regions. In the central highlands and the southwestern plateau, Pushtu predominates. In the northern plains, Dari, Uzbek, and Turkoman are spoken, whereas in the northeastern region, Dari and the various languages of the Dardic branch of the Indo-European family enjoy wider usage.

The nomadic way of life of many Afghans makes it necessary for them to speak more than one language. They have to travel to different regions of the country, not only with their herds but also for business.

Opposite: **An artisan restoring a carved signboard. The same Arabic alphabet is used for the main languages spoken in Afghanistan.**

Dari is used for communication between the different groups as most Afghans speak Dari. In the 1930s, during the reign of King Zahir Shah, the government tried to promote the use of Pushtu. For example, in 1936 Pushtu was declared the national language of Afghanistan. Dari, however, prevailed because of its importance in literature and because it is the language used by the business community of the country.

Various ancient Indo-European languages are spoken by small communities living in the Pamir Knots region in Badakhshan and in the Wakhan mountains. Among the more important groups are the Sughnis, the Wakhis, the Munjanis, and the Zebakis. Each local variant may have only several thousand speakers.

SHARED LANGUAGES

Most of the languages spoken in Afghanistan are also used in neighboring countries. Besides Dari, which shares its roots with Farsi, spoken in Iran, Uzbek and Turkoman are spoken in the former Central Asian republics of the Soviet Union. Many Pakistanis also speak Pushtu, and Baluchi is common to the Baluchi tribes who live in both Afghanistan and Pakistan. Tajiki, spoken by Tajiks, is a Dari dialect. It differs from standard Dari in pronunciation and is very similar to the Tajiki spoken in the former Soviet Union. Khorasani, spoken by Persians in the west and to the north of Kabul, is another Dari dialect.

The main Dari dialect found in Afghanistan is Kabuli, which is used by the majority of the educated elite. The structure of the Aimaq language is Iranian, but its vocabulary borrows heavily from Turkic languages. Hazaragi, spoken by the Hazaras, is a Dari dialect but also contains many Turkic and Mongol words.

Punjabi and Sindhi are the main Indian languages spoken in Afghanistan

by Hindus and Sikhs in the urban centers in eastern Afghanistan. Hindu merchants sometimes use Urdu as a language of trade.

All the different languages are again divided into dialects, each with a different pronunciation and vocabulary. Except in the case of extreme dialectical variation, most people speaking the same language can understand its dialects. Afghans who are not native Dari speakers usually know enough of the language to communicate with those speaking other languages.

SCRIPT

The many languages found in Afghanistan have a common factor: they are all written in the Arabic script, from right to left. The Arabic characters are supplemented, as needed, by the addition of diacritical marks to represent sounds that do not exist in Arabic. Because many languages in Afghanistan are related, anyone who has learned the expanded alphabet can read the script of these languages.

Some Pushtu, a little Dari, and perhaps a smattering of Uzbek and Turkoman are likely to enter the conversation of a group of Afghans bargaining at a sheep market.

The Friendly Hotel in Bamian displays English signs to attract English-speaking travelers. American Peace Corps volunteers once taught English to teachers in Afghanistan.

FOREIGN LANGUAGES

English, French, German, Italian, and Russian are spoken by some of the educated Afghans as these languages were taught in some schools. The literate among the Afghans can often speak not only a couple of other Afghan dialects besides their mother tongue, but also a few non-Afghan languages. It is not uncommon to meet officials who can speak as many as four or five languages, including English and Urdu.

Many Afghans who speak English acquired the language while working. Frequent contact between Afghans and the British in India have given the nomads and those who served in the army the ability to communicate in English. Many others learned English while working for Morrison-Knudsen, the U.S. company involved in the Helmand valley project and other U.S. ventures in Afghanistan during the 1950s.

THE PRESS IN AFGHANISTAN

The first newspaper in Afghanistan was published in the middle of the 19th century during the reign of Dost Mohammed. The Persian-language *Kabul*, later known as *Shams-un-Nahar*, published the latest happenings at the royal courts and lasted until 1879.

King Amanullah used the press to popularize his modernization campaign, and during his reign, no fewer than 15 newspapers were in circulation. Freedom of the press was provided by the constitution of 1931 and made more specific by Article 31 of the constitution of 1964. However, a new press law was enforced in 1965 that specified the conditions and limitations governing the publication of newspapers.

Today, the Government Printing House, under the supervision of the Ministry of Information and Culture, prints four daily newspapers in Kabul, including one in English. There are about a dozen other dailies, magazines, and periodicals published by various publishers, societies, and ministries, covering all the regions of Afghanistan.

Afghan radio transmits in Dari and Pushtu for 13 hours daily, and for three and a half hours in the other dialects. There is also a foreign service in Urdu, Arabic, English, German, and Russian for five and a half hours daily. Television broadcasts for five hours each day.

BODY LANGUAGE

Afghans use a great deal of body language in expressing themselves. There is also much physical contact among members of the same sex. Any touching between opposite sexes is strictly forbidden, in keeping with Islamic doctrine.

When greeting friends and acquaintances, Afghan men often clasp both hands in a firm handshake and hug and kiss each other on the cheeks to express warmth and camaraderie. Unlike in Western countries, they are not self-conscious walking arm-in-arm with other men.

In business dealings, contracts or agreements are sealed with a firm nodding of the head.

ARTS

AFGHANISTAN HAS A RICH cultural heritage covering more than 5,000 years. Little new or original art, literature, or architecture has been produced since the 17th century, when rivalry between the Persians and the Moghuls began. There has hardly been any prolonged period of peace in the country since then.

PRE-ISLAMIC HERITAGE

Archeological findings include the Rock and Pillar Edicts of Asoka the Great, which were erected to preach Buddhism and encourage pacifism by his subjects, and the ruins of the ancient Greek city at Ai Khanoum. It was in ancient Afghanistan that the artistic and architectural styles of the Greeks, Buddhists, and the Indus River civilizations fused to yield the Greco-Buddhist and Gandharan schools of art.

Opposite: **Exquisite tilework, dating from the Timurid period, in a mosque. The Timurid dynasty sparked off a brilliant revival of artistic and intellectual life in Afghanistan and Central Asia in the 15th and early 16th century.**

Left: **Buddhist frescoes discovered in the caves of Bamian. Buddhism, the religion founded by Gautama Buddha in India in the sixth century B.C., was first introduced in Afghanistan by rulers of the Mauryan empire.**

Above: **Intricate artwork on the Ghazni Victory Tower. The tower, which has survived almost a thousand years, was constructed during the reign of Mahmud of Ghazni (997–1030).**

Opposite: **The Friday Mosque in Herat. Parts of the mosque were damaged by bombing during the civil war.**

ISLAMIC HERITAGE

Afghanistan has played an important role in the development of Islamic culture. The greatest progress was made during the Ghaznavid era of the 10th and 11th centuries, and the Timurid era of the 14th and 15th centuries.

Mahmud of Ghazni summoned renowned men of learning to his court. Among those who came was Avicenna, a physician and philosopher. Avicenna is famous for his book, *Canon of Medicine*, which was used in medical schools in Europe before the 17th century. He also wrote many books on mathematics and astronomy. Also at Mahmud's court were 400 poets; among them was Firdausi, who composed the great epic *Shah-nama* (Book of Kings). Mahmud and his successors also built several magnificent mosques, palaces, and tombs.

The second great period of cultural development was at Herat under the Timurid rulers. Tamerlane and his successors ordered the construction of magnificent mosques and shrines. At Herat, Tamerlane established an elegant center of arts and learning.

ARCHITECTURE

Timurid architecture is characterized by its tall minarets, bulbous domes, and colorful tiles and is considered by scholars to be among the best in the world. Outstanding examples of such architecture found today include the Friday Mosque in Herat and the Blue Mosque of Mazar-e-Sharif.

The Blue Mosque was built in 1420 by Amir Hussein and is said to contain the remains of Ali, the son-in-law of the Prophet Mohammed. The dome is of pristine simplicity, in sharp contrast to the lushly patterned walls. The architecture consists of sharp, clear forms, and the entrance is through great portals that lead into an extensive courtyard. The entire building is enhanced by contrasting forms and textures.

To cover the walls, pieces of glazed tiles, in lapis lazuli, turquoise, deep green, yellow, black, and white, were carefully cut and fitted to form patterns of curving stems, leaves, and blossoms. Workmanship is so skilled that the panels appear to be painted, and the undulating surface causes the highly polished tiles to sparkle at certain angles.

Tilemakers skilled in this ancient art still live in Afghanistan today, and in times of peace, have been employed in restoration works.

LITERATURE

Novels are rare in Afghan literature. Poetry, however, is highly revered and popular in Afghanistan, and each ethnic group has its own poetry, epics, and songs. These were usually transmitted orally from generation to generation, sometimes by minstrels who went from village to village entertaining the patrons of teahouses and *caravanserais*.

The most popular theme in literature is war, followed by love and jealousy, then religion and folklore. Most stories express a religious sentiment, besides extolling certain virtues, such as courage.

Pushtun literature extols the warrior who dies for his principles. There are also many religious works in Pushtu, such as the *Makhzanul-Asrar* and the *Makhzanul-Islam*.

Kushal Khan Khattak and Abdur Rahman, who lived in the 17th century, are the most important Pushtu poets. Kushal Khan Khattak is considered the national poet of Afghanistan. He also wrote books on

THE TRAGIC TALE OF LEILA AND MAJNUN

The poignant romance of Leila, the daughter of a nomadic chief, and the poet Qais bin Amir, called Majnun ("Mad One") because his love cost him his sanity, has been told many times by poets, both as oral folklore and as literature. It is one of the most popular love stories from Turkey to the Malay archipelago in Southeast Asia.

In the story, after Majnun has been driven mad by his love for Leila, his father approaches Leila's father to arrange a marriage between his son and Leila but is refused because Majnun is mad. Leila ventures out in search of the wandering Majnun and is seen by Ibn Salam, a prince whom her father has compelled her to marry. The prince imprisons Leila, but she escapes and meets Majnun. Realizing he cannot marry her, Majnun sends her back, and she dies in grief. A brokenhearted Majnun dies embracing her gravestone and is buried beside her.

CRITICIZING RELIGIOUS BIGOTRY

The knowing, the perceptive man
Is he who knows about himself,
For in self-knowledge and insight
Lies knowledge of the Holiest.
If in his heart there is no fear,
His deeds are not those of the good,
Pay no heed to one who's skilled
In quoting the Koran by heart.

— A poem by Kushal Khan Khattak

philosophy, ethics, medicine, and an autobiography. He is held in great awe by the Afghans as he was not only a great poet but also a warrior. Although constantly at war with the Moghuls or other Pushtun tribes, the Khattak chieftain wrote great poetry about war, love, and life.

Baluchi poetry paints vivid pictures of the Baluchis' countryside and life, and nature is a favorite theme. Generosity is exalted and greed condemned.

Turkic literature is shared by all its diverse tribes. The magically swift horse, the faithful companion, and a hero possessing superhuman qualities are very common themes. Some of their epics that are now a shared heritage are the Uzbek *Alpamysh, Koblandy, Yer-Targyn*, and *Yedigy*, and the Kirghiz *Manas*. The poem *Kudatkybilik* by Balasgun is held to be an outstanding example of Turkic literature. Balasgun's philosophy is said to be on par with that of Avicenna.

Persian literature is well known to the educated, and odes and ballads have been transmitted orally through the generations. Children are told tales from *Kalilah wa Dimnah*, a collection of animal stories very like Aesop's fables. Also popular are tragic love stories, similar to Shakespeare's *Romeo and Juliet*, the most famous of these being *Leila and Majnun, Adam and Durkhani, Farhad and Shirin*, and *Yusof and Zulekha*.

Contemporary prose and poetry are written in Dari and often imitate the classical Persian style and format. In 1947, a literary-political society called Awakening Youth was formed, and for a time, there was a period of greater freedom of expression among authors.

When Kushal Khan Khattak died in 1694, he left behind a considerable body of work, and many of his poems have since been translated by Pushtu scholars. Kushal Khan Khattak's grandson, Afdal Khan, later wrote a history of the Pushtuns.

A painted wall in a tea-
house in Kunduz. Afghan
paintings often express
a mood, rather than at-
tempt realistic imagery.

VISUAL ARTS

Artists in Afghanistan were greatly influenced by the works of Bizhad, from
the Timurid period in Herat. It was the Herat school of manuscript
illumination that developed a miniature style combining great technical
skill with studied naturalism. Paintings consisted of precise and clear
shapes in brilliant colors. Human, animal, and cloud forms were stylized,
creating a tapestry-like effect.

No great sculptor or painter has emerged in Afghanistan since then, and
of the graphic arts, only calligraphy and illumination have survived. This,
however, is no longer a profitable employment since the introduction of
printing.

An arts college, Maktab-i-Sanai, was established in the 1930s, where an
annual exposition was held; most of the works were oil paintings or water
colors. Two outstanding painters during the 1960s were Abdul Ghaffour
Breshna and Khair Mohamed.

THEATER AND MOVIES

Original Persian plays, or those adapted from European classics or Arabic and Turkish comedies, are shown at the few theaters in Kabul, Herat, and Kandahar. Traveling companies take plays to the provincial towns and perform at local fairs.

Women's roles are often played by men, and most actors are amateurs. Among the European classics, the adaptations of Moliere's comedies are very popular. Occasionally, Shakespeare's plays are also adapted.

Movie theaters usually show Indian movies, especially those in Hindi, and Pakistani movies.

A wall painting of a mosque. Afghan art reached its peak in the 15th century when Herat became the center of a noted school of miniaturists, who illustrated poetical and historical works.

LEISURE

AFGHANS TAKE GAMES and sports very seriously. Winning in sports is, to the Afghan, of utmost importance as a match is not just a friendly joust but a question of personal, tribal, and family honor.

Games are often held during festivals and celebrations and draw huge crowds of spectators.

GAMES OF CHILDHOOD

Childhood ends early in Afghanistan, for the children have little time to play. Their games are simple. In rural Afghanistan, a little girl's toy may be a crudely carved doll made by her father, and her brother may play with a slingshot. Children also play *buzul-bazi* ("boo-jool-BAWH-jee"), a game resembling marbles, but using sheep knucklebones.

Opposite: **The competitive spirit of Afghans is evident in their leisure activities, which include pitting animals against each other for sport. Cockfights are common, but any animal may be used: partridges, dogs, goats, or even camels. The spectators bet on the outcome of the fight.**

Left: **Adult responsibilities begin early in Afghanistan. Household chores, such as washing up after a meal, must be completed before these children can run off to play.**

A game of *buzkashi* in progress. *Buzkashi* is, by far, the most exciting Afghan national sport.

BUZKASHI

Buzkashi ("BOOZ-kah-SHEE") is to the Afghans what baseball is to the Americans. The game is believed to have been developed in Central Asia and the plains of Mongolia. It plays a major role in the lives of the people of northern Afghanistan. For the farmer and the nomad, it is a reminder of a heroic ancestry. The game is often played during the *Now Ruz* ("neh-ROHZ") festival in March. Only men participate in *buzkashi*.

Buzkashi literally means "grab the goat," but these days calves are more commonly used. The headless carcass of a calf is placed in the center of a circle formed by two teams of horsemen. Teams have been known to consist of as many as 1,000 players. When the signal is given, the riders move to the center, and each tries to lift the carcass onto his horse.

This is no mean task in the midst of flailing hoofs, slashing whips, and the weight of the carcass. Horse and rider move in perfect harmony and are a joy to watch. Despite the potentially dangerous situation, injuries seldom occur as the horses are extremely well trained and their hoofs never land on a fallen rider.

Once the calf is on his saddle, the rider secures the calf's legs under his own. He must then ride to a point one to three miles away, return to the starting point, and drop the calf where he picked it up. Only then is he said to have scored a goal. During all this time, the other riders try to snatch the calf away from him.

The horses, ridden by the master players, or *chapandaz* ("CHAWP-hehn-DAHZ"), who control the game, must be trained for at least five years. Rules are laid down by the Afghan Olympic Federation, and two types of fouls have been introduced—hitting an opponent intentionally with one's whip or forcing him off his horse. Flagrant defiance of these rules means expulsion from the game, forcing the team to be one man short.

The rules also limit the duration of the game to an hour with a 10-minute break at half-time, and the teams now consist of no more than 10 players each. These rules are followed only at official games. *Buzkashi* played by the tribes, especially those in the north, is as full of thrills and spills as ever.

The Uzbeks, Tajiks, and Turkomans play buzkashi, *but the best players are the Uzbeks, who are acknowledged as the* buzkashi *champions of Afghanistan.*

THE AFGHAN HOUND

Afghan hounds are commonly reared in Afghanistan and are used for hunting. They are known as *tazi* ("TAWH-zee") and have shorter hair than their counterparts bred in the United States and Europe.

Despite their name, these hounds actually originated in Egypt thousands of years ago and became renowned only after being developed as hunters in the rugged terrain of Afghanistan.

Afghan hounds are highly valued by their owners for their hunting prowess. Afghans use the hounds to track down gazelle, goats, snow leopards, and bears. Marco Polo sheep and ducks are also popular game.

PAHLWANI AND OTHER SPORTS

Most games native to Afghanistan are violent and vigorous. Wrestling, or *pahlwani* ("pehl-wah-NI"), is popular with men all over the country. The rules are simple—the wrestler can grab the arms or the clothing of his opponent but must not touch his legs. Usually, wrestlers grab their opponent's forearm, moving sideways in a crablike, rocking motion, trying to catch their adversary off balance.

A man will leap high to try to toss his opponent, who in turn will twist in midair, ending behind the other man and holding him in a headlock. When one man has been thrown to the ground and his shoulders pinned, the winner is lifted waist high by his coach and carried around the field to the cheers of the crowd.

In Nuristan, the men and boys play a game resembling rugby. The two teams each stand in a row, one row of players facing the other. One man from each team tries to dash past the opposing team, whose players try to block him. This bone-shaking game consists of a great deal of pushing and tripping.

King Habibullah, during his reign (1901–1919), introduced some Western sports, such as tennis, golf, and cricket, and built several golf courses in Afghanistan. After World War II, other team sports were introduced in the country. Their spirit of preserving honor makes the Afghans excel at such games as basketball, soccer, and field hockey.

MUSIC AND DANCING

The Afghans love to sing and dance. In the evenings, young men get together to sing and to play music. Afghans even sing while they work or travel.

Afghans take a break from the hard work of building houses for some spontaneous dancing in the streets. Traditional dances and music help preserve cultural values in a population that is largely illiterate.

Musicians are not well respected, but it is socially acceptable for Afghans to play music for their own entertainment. Performances of Indian music are well patronized in the cities. Before the Saur Revolution in 1978, the attitude toward women was more liberal, and Afghan singers such as Roxane and Sermand were popular.

The music of the mountains is purely Afghan: simple yet vigorous, resembling the flamenco music of Spain. In the cities, the songs have a strong Indian influence and also often reflect Western trends.

Although different in many aspects, Afghan music is closer to Western music than any other music in Asia. Their orchestras consists of a number of string instruments, drums, and a small hand-pumped harmonium.

Men dance at weddings and at festivals. They usually dance with their swords and guns, in ever-widening circles. The older men form an inner circle, the younger men dance in the middle, and horsemen dance on the outside. The music starts on a slow beat and picks up tempo as the dance progresses, until the music and the dancers reach a frenzy. The music then ceases abruptly, and after a short break, the dancing and music begin again. During Pushtun weddings, men and women dance in rows of 10 to 12 people, each waving a brightly colored scarf above the head.

FESTIVALS

AS IN MOST OTHER MUSLIM COUNTRIES, many holidays in Afghanistan celebrate the important events in the Islamic calendar. These holidays are usually marked with special prayers and sermons in mosques. Many Afghans also take the opportunity to visit relatives or entertain with lavish meals. Independence Day and Revolution Day are the two most important secular holidays in Afghanistan.

EID AL-FITR

The most important month in the Islamic calendar is Ramadan, the ninth month, during which every Muslim, except the old, the sick, young children, and pregnant women, is required to avoid food, drink, and tobacco from dawn to dusk.

Fasting is called *ruzah* ("roo-ZAH") in Afghanistan. Most Afghans break their daily fast by eating dates or raisins before their customary evening meal and tea. Because the Islamic calendar is a lunar calendar, Ramadan occurs 11 days earlier each year; fasting can be arduous when it falls in the summer. In 1995, Ramadan coincided with the month of February. During Ramadan, all activity slows down during the day, and the people liven up only after dusk falls.

The feast of *Eid al-Fitr* ("ID ahl-fitter," also known as *Shaber-i-Bairam,* "shah-herh-REE-bai-RAHM," in Turkic and *Qamqai Akhta,* "kahm-kah-yee ekh-TAH," in Pushtu) commences after the month of fasting ends, on the first day of the month of Shawal.

Celebrations usually last for about three days. Congregational prayers are held in mosques, after which Afghans visit their friends and relatives. New clothes, especially for the children, are made, and much food is prepared.

Opposite: **A man in quiet prayer during the month of Ramadan. Some devout Afghans observe the Ramadan fast so strictly that they will not even swallow saliva during their fast.**

EID AL-ADHA

Once the fasting month and ensuing celebrations have ended, it is time for those planning to perform their obligatory pilgrimage to Mecca to start preparations for their journey. The *hajj*, or pilgrimage, takes place in the 12th month of the Muslim calendar, the rituals being performed in Mecca between the seventh and the 10th days. Those who have made the pilgrimage are referred to, respectfully, as *hajjis* ("HAW-jees"), if male, and *hajjahs* ("HAW-jahs"), if female.

A feast known as *Eid al-Adha* ("ID ahl-ehd-HAH") in the Muslim world is celebrated on the 10th day of the month. Animals, such as sheep, goats, and camels, are sacrificed, especially by those who have already performed the *hajj*. This commemorates the slaying of a sheep, instead of Isaac, as a sacrifice by his father Abraham, at the command of Allah. One third of the slaughtered animal is used by the family, another third is distributed to relatives, and the rest is given to the poor. This feast of the sacrifice is also referred to as *Eid al-Qurban* ("ID ahl-koor-BAHN"). In Turkic, it is known as *buyuk bairam* ("boo-yook bai-RAHM").

ASHURA

To the Shi'ites, the most important religious period of the year is the first 10 days of the new year. This is a period of mourning, in memory of the killing of Hussein, the grandson of Prophet Mohammed, at Karbala on October 10, 680, along with 72 of his immediate family and followers. The festival climaxes on the 10th day of the month of Muharram ("MAW-heh-rahm"), called *Ashura* ("ah-SHOO-rah").

Ashura is an optional fast day. As the Shi'ite population is relatively small, this day is celebrated on a smaller scale in Afghanistan than in

countries with large Shi'ite populations, such as neighboring Iran. Mourners in Iran join a procession through the streets, giving themselves over to frenzied expressions of grief, beating themselves, and sometimes even drawing blood.

BIRTH OF MOHAMMED

Muslims also celebrate the birth of the Prophet Mohammed, who was born on the 12th day of the month of Rabiul Awal. It is one of the most important holidays in Afghanistan, and prayers and feasting continue for weeks afterward. In the home, stories are told about Mohammed's life, his parents, and his birth. Religious leaders may also remind worshipers of their duties as Muslims.

The Prophet is believed to have died on the same day, adding significance to the importance and solemnity of the feast.

The mosque is the focal point of most religious festivals. Besides the special congregational prayers conducted on these occasions, mosque officials organize the slaughter of animals and distribution of meat during *Eid al-Adha* and the collection of a tax from Muslims during *Eid al-Fitr*, as well as its subsequent distribution to the poor.

NOW RUZ

Literally meaning a new day, *Now Ruz* is the first day of spring and of the Afghan solar calendar, and falls on March 21. This festival dates back to the time when Zoroastrianism was still a powerful religion, long before Islam arrived in Afghanistan. *Now Ruz* was once celebrated on June 21, or the solar equinox, but the date was later changed by the Achaemenids to the present date.

Several ancient superstitions are associated with the New Year. For example, Afghans believe that on *Now Ruz*, an ugly old woman called Ajuzak roams the world. If rain falls on that day, it is a sign that Ajuzak is washing her hair and the coming year's harvest will be bountiful. Infants are hidden to protect them from Ajuzak's evil eye.

During the celebrations, lavish meals are prepared in Afghan homes. Two dishes, *samanak* ("seh-meh-NAHK") and *haft-mewah* ("hehft-meh-WAH"), are specially cooked for the occasion. *Samanak*, a dessert made of wheat and sugar, can take more than two days to prepare. *Haft-mewah* consists of seven fruits and nuts to symbolize spring: walnuts, almonds, pistachios, red and green raisins, dried apricots, and a local fruit known as *sanje* ("sehn-JEE").

On *Now Ruz*, the ceremonial raising of the flag at the tomb of Ali, Prophet Mohammed's son-in-law, is held at Mazar-e-Sharif. The standard of Ali is raised in the courtyard, and the devout touch the staff—a tradition known as *jandah bala kardan* ("jehn-DAH baw-loh kahr-DAHN")—hoping to gain merit. The staff remains standing for 40 days, during which thousands of pilgrims flock to Mazar-e-Sharif, including the sick and crippled, hoping to be cured. Forty days after *Now Ruz*, on the day the flag is lowered in Mazar-e-Sharif, a distinctive red species of tulip blooms and then disappears soon after.

JESHN

One of the few holidays without religious significance in Afghanistan is *Jeshn* ("JEH-shen"), or Independence Day. This is usually a week-long celebration to mark Afghanistan's independence from the British in May 1919, after the Third Anglo-Afghan War.

Because the Treaty of Rawalpindi, which granted Afghanistan the freedom to conduct its own foreign affairs, was signed in August, and also because the harvest ends only in August, giving the rural population more freedom from work to participate in the festivities, celebrations are usually held at the end of August.

OTHER HOLIDAYS

Besides Independence Day, Afghanistan also observes Workers' Day, or Labor Day, which is also a national holiday in many other countries, on the first of May.

NATIONAL HOLIDAYS OF AFGHANISTAN

First day of Ramadan	varies
Eid al-Fitr (end of Ramadan)	varies
Now Ruz (New Year's Day)	March 21
Revolution Day	April 27
Workers' Day	May 1
Eid al-Adha (Feast of the Sacrifice)	varies
Ashura (martyrdom of Hussein)	varies
Birth of Prophet Mohammed	varies
Independence Day	August 18

The national holiday of Revolution Day marks the date, April 27, 1978, on which President Daoud was overthrown. Besides the mandatory military parades and displays, buzkashi *matches are held and attended by huge crowds of spectators. All this happens during periods of peace, which have been rare in recent years.*

FOOD

AFGHAN CUISINE IS A BLEND of the cooking styles of many groups that invaded and occupied Afghanistan throughout the centuries. The strongest influences come from its neighbors, Iran and India.

Both Iranian food, often regarded as the most refined of all Middle Eastern cuisines, and Indian food, probably the most sophisticated in South Asia, have had the advantage of thousands of years to develop and mature. Afghans have incorporated the best elements of the foods of these ancient civilizations into their own cuisine.

Afghan food is a delightful cuisine that is neither too spicy nor too bland. The staples of its cuisine are rice and the bread called *naan* ("nawn").

Opposite: **Food is cooked communally by the Kirghiz tribes in the Wakhan.**

Left: **An enterprising young Afghan sells freshly prepared food. The Afghan diet excludes pork, which is forbidden by Islam.**

Kabul street vendors with cartloads of *naan* for sale. *Naan* is also a favorite food in neighbouring countries like Iran, Pakistan, and India.

NAAN

Naan is a round, flat bread that resembles oversized pancakes. It is made from every kind of grain that can be ground into flour, even peas and mulberries.

It is usually baked in a *tandur* ("tehn-DOOR"), or clay pot, which is buried in the ground with hot coals at the bottom; it can also be baked on a hot, circular iron griddle. The nomads often bake it on heated stones. *Naan* can be baked in different shapes, too. Oblong is a common shape, although in the north, oval *naan* is the norm.

Naan is usually baked plain. Sometimes a filling, such as leeks or potatoes, is added for variety.

This staple is especially important in the villages, where Afghans generally consume more bread than their counterparts in the towns. Town dwellers, who have access to a wider variety of food, consume larger amounts of rice and meat.

PILAU

Several varieties of rice grow in the wetter areas of Afghanistan, including Kunduz, Jalalabad, and Laghman, and meals with rice are as common as those with *naan*. Rice may be served plain with side dishes, but on special occasions, *pilau* ("pah-LAO"), or rice cooked with meats or vegetables, is served. A guest to an Afghan's home is invariably invited to share a meal of *pilau*. The Afghans cook the rice with clarified butter (called *ghee* in Hindi), lard from the tail of a fat-tailed sheep, or vegetable shortening.

Shorwa *("shoor-WAH"), a gravy usually made with mutton stock, is a favorite dish. Afghans dip their* naan *in it or drink it as a soup. In the north, the Uzbek make their gravy with cattle blood and tomatoes.*

PILAU GALORE!

The number of ways *pilau* can be cooked is limited only by the chef's imagination. The more popular varieties in Afghanistan are:

Chilaw ("cheh-LAO")	Plain rice with a large hunk of mutton or chicken buried within the mound of rice.
Qabli ("KAW-blee")	*Pilau* with raisins, shredded carrot, almonds, and pistachios. A guest served *qabli* is held in great respect.
Sabzi ("SEHB-zee")	*Pilau* with spinach.
Mashong ("maw-SHOHNG")	*Pilau* with small green peas.
Yakhni ("YEHKH-nee")	*Pilau* with mutton in steamed rice.
Reshta ("REHSH-tah")	*Pilau* with eggs.
Bonjan-i-sia ("baw-JAW-nee-SI-yah")	*Pilau* with eggplant.
Morgh ("MOORGH")	*Pilau* with chicken.
Naranj ("NAW-rehnj")	Sweetish *pilau* with dried orange peel.
Kala-pacheh ("KAH-la-PAH-cheh")	*Pilau* with the head (including eyeballs) and feet of a sheep.
Landi ("LOON-dee")	*Pilau* with dried meat prepared like jerky; a favorite winter dish.

Pilau is usually served with a side dish of vegetables and yogurt. Popular vegetables are squash, carrots, eggplants, spinach, potatoes, and peas. Sometimes pickled vegetables, called *torshi* ("TOHR-shee"), are also served. In Kabul and Jalalabad, a special hot chili sauce, *chutney-morch* ("CHOOT-nee-moorch"), is a favorite.

KEBAB

Kebabs ("KAY-babs") are another favorite food of the Afghans. These are usually small cubes of meat skewered with onions, tomatoes, and pieces of fat, then grilled over open charcoal broilers.

As with *pilaus*, there are many different varieties of *kebabs*. One of the most popular types is *kofta* ("kohf-TAH") *kebab*, which is made with minced meat ground with onions. Another much-loved version is *shami* ("SHAW-mee") *kebab*—minced meat mixed with beaten eggs and mashed potatoes before broiling.

OTHER FOODS

The Uzbek, Tajik, and other Afghans in the north enjoy pasta dishes, such as *ash* ("ashk"), a minestrone-type noodle soup. They also have several types of ravioli, called *ashak* ("ashk-HAK"), with a variety of fillings, from cheese to meat and leeks. A steamed meat dumpling, called *mantu* ("MAHN-too"), similar to that found in Tibet, is eaten in the north, especially in the winter.

Dairy products are a staple part of the Afghans' diet, especially nomads and those in rural areas. Milk not only from cows, but also goats and sheep, is drunk. Besides milk and yogurt, many different types of cheese, both pasteurized and unpasteurized, are consumed.

Poultry, including chickens, ducks, turkeys, and guinea fowls, and eggs are also popular. Freshwater fish from Afghanistan's many rivers has become increasingly popular in recent years. In addition, game or small birds, a prize treat, are hunted and cooked.

Many of Afghanistan's sweets and desserts are similar to those found in India and Pakistan. Besides these, both fresh and dry fruits are abundant. Fruits are of the Mediterranean and temperate variety and include melons, apples, pears, apricots, cherries, mulberries, and plums. Nuts, such as pistachios, almonds, and walnuts, are a major part of the Afghan diet and are often carried for quick snacks.

Rice is also cooked and served in several ways in addition to the *pilau* varieties. In convalescence, it is eaten as *kichri* ("KEEK-ree"), or *shuleh* ("SHOO-lah"), which is a gruel of rice and split green peas. This is usually served with a mixture of minced meat and ghee or sour cream.

A pudding called *faluda* ("faw-loo-DAH") is prepared by steaming a mixture of wheat flour and milk in a porous bag for 10 to 12 hours. This is served with boiled rice spaghetti and syrup.

A favorite Afghan rice dish is dampok *("DAHM-pok"), which is simply rice boiled with oil and water.*

119

TEA

Tea is the national drink in Afghanistan and is extremely popular in a land where the consumption of alcohol is prohibited by Islam. It is not only served with meals but also drunk in between meals.

Two types of tea are commonly drunk in Afghanistan—black tea south of the Hindu Kush and green tea in the north. Both teas are served in the teahouses found in towns and villages throughout the country, where Afghan men gather to drink tea and while away their leisure time.

Sugar is considered a luxury, and Afghans have to pay extra to sweeten their tea. Many Afghans soak a sugar cube in the tea, then either eat it or hold it to their mouth as they drink the tea.

Unlike many other people in South Asia, most Afghans prefer their tea without any milk.

COOK A ONE-POT AFGHAN MEAL

Recipe for yakhni pilau

1 pound (500 g) basmati rice
3 green peppers
8 ounces (250 g) tomatoes
10 ounces (300 g) onions
8 ounces (250 g) ginger
5 cloves garlic
2 tablespoons ghee (clarified butter; if unavailable, use butter)
1 stick cinnamon
10 cloves
1 pound (500 g) mutton, cut in large cubes
2 teaspoons salt
2 cups yogurt

Clean the rice, washing it and changing the water until it is clear. Let it soak for about half an hour.

Cut the peppers and the tomatoes into bite-size pieces. Peel and slice the onions. Grind the ginger and garlic into a smooth paste.

Heat the ghee in a deep saucepan. When hot, drop in the cinnamon and cloves. Add the onion slices and fry until the onion is light brown.

Add the ginger and garlic paste and stir for a couple of minutes, then add the mutton and salt. Brown the meat.

Put in the peppers and tomatoes. Add the yogurt, cover the saucepan, and simmer gently. If the liquid dries up, add water.

When the mutton is cooked to medium rare, add about three cups of water, and bring the liquid to a boil.

Drain all the water from the rice and add the rice to the saucepan. The stock must be at least two inches (five centimeters) above the level of the rice. Add more water if necessary, and boil until almost dry.

Cover the pot tightly and leave to cook on very low heat until completely dry. Serve immediately.

In Afghanistan, as in other Muslim countries, animals must be slaughtered according to prescribed Islamic rituals before their meat can be eaten.

AFGHANISTAN

A **B** **C** **D**

1

2

3

4

CHINA

TAJIKISTAN

TURKMENISTAN

UZBEKISTAN

Amudar'ya

Sher Khan
Bandar

*Amudar'ya
Bridge*

Kunduz

Kokcha

Qala
Panja

Ishkashim

*Baroghil
Pass*

Sheberghan

Balkh

Mazar-e-Sharif

Kunduz

Baghlan

Pol-e-Khomri

*Nowshak
(24,557 ft / 7,482m)*

*Dorah-An
Pass*

Meymaneh

*Band-i
Amur*

*Salang
Pass*

Panjshir

Paropamisus

Hari Rud

Bamian

Shah Fuladi

Kuh-e

-Baba

*Shibar
Pass*

Charikar

Kabul

KABUL

Jalalabad

Safed Koh

*Khyber
Pass*

Herat

Hazarajat

Helmand

Farah Rud

Ghazni

INDIA

Farah

Tarnak

Arghandab

Dasht-i-Khash

Kandahar

Lake Helmand

Dori

*Sistan
Basin*

Dasht-i-Margo

Helmand

Registan

Gaud-i-Zirreh

Chagai Hills

IRAN

PAKISTAN

● Capital city
● Major town
▲ Mountain Peak

Feet		Meters
16,500		5,000
9,900		3,000
6,600		2,000
3,300		1,000
1,650		500
660		200
0		0

Scale 1:8,500,000

0	50	100	150 Miles
0	50 100 150 200	250 Kilometers	

122

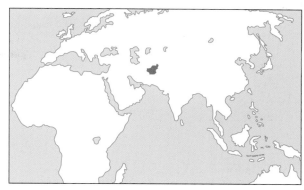

QUICK NOTES

AREA
264,000 square miles (683,760 square kilometers)

POPULATION
21.7 million (1993 estimate)

CAPITAL
Kabul

OFFICIAL NAME
Islamic State of Afghanistan

OFFICIAL LANGUAGES
Pushtu, Dari

PROVINCES
Badakhshan, Badghis, Baghlan, Balkh, Bamian, Farah, Faryab, Ghazni, Ghor, Helmand, Herat, Jowzjan, Kabul, Kandahar, Kapisa, Konarha, Kunduz, Laghman, Logar, Nangarhar, Nimroze, Paktia, Paktika, Parwan, Samangan, Takhar, Uruzgan, Wardak, Zabul

HIGHEST POINT
Nowshak (24,557 feet / 7,482 meters)

MAJOR LAKES
Lake Helmand, Gaud-i-Zirreh

MAJOR RELIGION
Sunni Islam

MAJOR RIVERS
Helmand, Amudar'ya, Hari Rud, Kabul

MAJOR CITIES
Kandahar, Mazar-e-Sharif, Herat, Ghazni, Jalalabad, Farah, Sheberghan, Charikar, Kunduz, Meymaneh, Pol-e-Khomri

NATIONAL FLAG
Three bands—black, white, and green, inscribed with "God is great" and "There is no other God but Allah and Mohammed is his Prophet."

CURRENCY
1 afghani = 100 puls
US$1 = 1,826 afghanis

MAIN EXPORTS
Karakul skins and wool, cotton, dried fruit and nuts, fresh fruit, natural gas

POLITICAL LEADERS
Ahmad Shah—founder of the Afghan state in 1747
Dost Mohammed—king in 1826–1839 and 1842–1863
Zahir Shah—the last king of Afghanistan (1933–1973)
Babrak Karmal—president (1979–1986)
Sayid Mohammed Najibullah—president (1987–1992)
Burhanuddin Rabbani—president since 1992

ANNIVERSARIES
Revolution Day (April 27)
Independence Day (August 18)

GLOSSARY

azan ("eh-ZAHN")
The call to prayer.

bad-i-sad-o-bist-roz
("bawh-dee-sah-doh-bist-ROHZ")
Strong winds along the Iran-Afghanistan border.

buzkashi ("BOOZ-kah-SHEE")
Game in which teams of horsemen try to drag a headless calf over a goal line.

caravanserais ("korh-VOHN-seh-ROI")
Inns found in towns.

chadri ("chaw-dree")
Traditional clothes, worn in public, covering a woman from head to foot.

chaykhana ("chaw-KHAH-nah")
Teahouse.

hajj ("HAHJ")
Pilgrimage to Mecca.

jangal ("jehng-EHL")
Wild pigs.

jihad ("jee-HAHD")
The permanent struggle to make the word of Allah supreme.

juy ("joo-YEE")
Artificially made pools or streams.

Loya Jirgah ("law-yah jorh-GAH")
Great Assembly.

mahi-kholdar ("maw-hee-KHOOL-darh")
Trout found in rivers north of the Hindu Kush.

Meli Shura ("MEH-li-SHOO-rah")
Highest legislative body of Afghanistan.

mujahedin ("moo-JAH-hee-DEEN")
Holy warriors of Islam.

mullah ("mool-LAH")
Muslim teacher or scholar.

naan ("nawn")
Roundish flat bread, a staple food in Afghanistan.

pahlwani ("pehl-wah-NI")
Wrestling.

pilau ("pah-LAO")
Rice cooked with meats or vegetables.

purdah ("perhr-DAH")
Veil for Muslim women.

Pushtunwalli ("PUHSH-toon-WAH-lee")
Code of conduct upheld by Afghans.

salat ("saw-LAWT")
Prayers.

sawm ("SAWM")
The act of fasting during the month of Ramadan.

shahadat ("sheh-hah-DEHT")
The belief in Allah as the only God, and in the Prophet Mohammed as His messenger.

tandur ("tehn-DOOR")
Clay pot used to bake *naan*.

Wolasi Jirgah ("woo-LAW-si jorh-GAH")
House of Representatives.

yurt ("yerht")
Tent used by seminomads.

zakat ("zeh-KAHT")
Alms given to the poor every year.

BIBLIOGRAPHY

Ansary, Mir T. *Afghanistan: Fighting for Freedom*. New York: Macmillan Children's Book Group, 1991.

Clifford, Mary L. *The Land and People of Afghanistan*. New York: Harper Collins Children's Books, 1989.

Herda, D.J. *Afghan Rebels*. New York: Franklin Watts, 1990.

Lerner Publications. *Afghanistan in Pictures*. Minneapolis, 1989.

Michael, Roland, and Michaud, Sabrina. *Afghanistan*. New York: Thames and Hudson, 1990.

INDEX

INDEX

INDEX